MW00328622

SMASH THE FUNNEL

"My core business is helping companies with increased revenue generation. *Smash the Funnel* is now in my arsenal. I recommend you do the same."

—Jack Daly, three-time Amazon number-one-best-selling author and six-time serial entrepreneur

. . .

"In my experience, everyone wants to jump to the tactics and shortcut the strategy. Eric and Mike's new book boils sales, marketing, and client-service strategy down to a simple-to-understand methodology that any salesperson or marketer can use to get better results. I really appreciated the practical application of each of the eight stages of the Cyclonic Buyer Journey, supported by the tactics and the metrics that go with each stage. If you are looking for a way to think differently about sales and marketing, this book is a must-have."

—Ben Kirshner, CEO of Elite SEM

. . .

"*Smash the Funnel* is a must-read for any company wanting to grow sales. The insights in this book offer a fresh approach that I can't wait to put to work!"

—Mo Fathelbab, president of Forum Resources Network and author of *The Friendship Advantage*

"I have read many marketing books over the years. There are a handful that have a marked impact on the way I approach and think about demand generation. *Smash the Funnel* is one of those books. It creates an excellent model for keeping marketers focused on the most important part of driving revenue: the buyer's mindset. Through real-world stories and interesting historical tidbits, the authors make a strong case for taking a fresh look at the demand-generation funnel."

—Mitchell Rose, VP of Strategic Partnerships at Billtrust

. . .

"*Smash the Funnel* provides actionable strategies that show you how to break the bottlenecks that add costs and friction to your selling process. If you want to predictably increase sales, while significantly reducing your cost per sale, then you must read this book! Mike and Eric completely rewrote the rules of sales and marketing. The book is fun and in-your-face. This book shatters your current paradigm of what effective sales and marketing is. You will walk away with practical, actionable tools that will help you make more money for your organization! Mike and Eric promised me 'NO Fluff' when they handed me this book, and boy did they deliver! This book is REAL and USEFUL!"

—Barrett Ersek, CEO of Holganix

"Back in 2008, I read Mike and Eric's first book, *Reality Marketing Revolution*, and called it 'a great how-to marketing book.' They have come a long way! In their new book, this contrarian duo attacks the long-standing concept of the sales funnel and presents a new way to think about driving revenue through sales, marketing, and ongoing delivery: the Cyclonic Buyer Journey. *Smash the Funnel* takes the reader step-by-step through the eight cycles that identify the stages sales and marketing practitioners must consider if they want to achieve the results they are seeking. While academic in its voice, Eric and Mike took the extra step and created a fable to represent a company (like yours) that applied this new strategy and transitioned from 'old-school thinking' to this progressive Cyclonic Buyer's Journey. From the strategists to the tacticians, all sales and marketing professionals will get huge value for their organization from this book."

—Verne Harnish, founder of Entrepreneurs' Organization (EO) and author of *Scaling Up (Rockefeller Habits 2.0)*

. . .

"*Smash the Funnel* is the new bible for revenue growth. Its approach to strategy, tactics, analytics, and technology make it a must-read for CEOs, CMOs, sales leaders, and anyone wondering why their company is not growing—or not growing fast enough. It literally uncovers the key reasons and provides solutions that produce the growth you're looking for. Get it, read it, and start following it today."

—Pete Caputa, CEO of Databox

"*Smash the Funnel* is an insightful read that surfaces the difficulties marketers face with traditional frameworks. When we attempt to box in the customer journey, we forget that boxes can break easily. In defining the cyclone, Mike and Eric have shed light on the invisible—and often convoluted—path customers take toward a conversion. The book is a useful and enjoyable read from two digital marketers with their pulse on the ever-changing marketing landscape."

—Franco Valentino, CEO of Narrative SEO

. . .

"This is one of the best marketing—no, revenue growth—books of the year. Finally, someone is saying what we all know. Driving revenue consistently is complex. Mike and Eric uncover why and, most importantly, what to do about it. Their innovative new model for revenue generation, the Cyclonic Buyer Journey, is the ultimate roadmap for marketing, sales, and customer-service executives to start proactively attacking revenue growth."

—Sangram Vajre, cofounder and CTO of Terminus

. . .

"*Smash the Funnel* sets the tone for how CEOs should be thinking about revenue generation going forward. The Cyclonic Buyer Journey is the new map business leaders need to more effectively deploy marketing and sales tactics."

—Don Doctor, partner at Cramer Mountain Growth Capital

SMASH

THE

FUNNEL

THE CYCLONIC BUYER JOURNEY

A New Map for Sustainable, Repeatable,
Predictable Revenue Generation

ERIC KEILES & MIKE LIEBERMAN

AN INC.
ORIGINAL.

An Inc. Original
New York, New York
www.inc.com

Distributed by River Grove Books

Design and composition by Greenleaf Book Group
Cover design by Greenleaf Book Group
Cover imagery ©iStockphoto.com/kaho0818 and Runrun2, 2018. Used under license from Shutterstock.com

Publisher's Cataloging-in-Publication data is available.

Print ISBN: 978-0-9991913-9-2

eBook ISBN: 978-1-7325102-0-3

First Edition

All men can see these tactics whereby I conquer, but what none can see is the strategy out of which victory is evolved.

—SUN TZU, *THE ART OF WAR*

CONTENTS

FOREWORD

I've been using the sales funnel for twenty-eight years, my whole career. This year, I retired the funnel—threw it a party, gave it a gold watch, and congratulated it on its move to a condo in Naples, Florida.

It was the right thing to do. The funnel failed to keep up with the times.

Since the beginning of this decade, Mike and Eric's company, Square 2 Marketing, has been a partner with my company, HubSpot. They too have lived—and out-lived—the funnel, and they have the stories to prove it! *Smash the Funnel* is jammed with stories full of behaviors that made perfect sense in a funnel world but are now, in the era of what they call the cyclone, woefully deficient or flat-out counterproductive. Each anecdote deals a crushing dent to or shows a fatal crack in the funnel; you'll read each with an equal measure of self-awareness, laughter, and cringing.

Too often, customer delight is something businesses think happens after the sale, as the responsibility of the customer service department. Don't get me wrong: I'm all in favor of investing in quality customer service. But an overall customer experience begins even before that first customer touch—and can fly or fail at any point, even with seemingly inert activities such as billing, packaging, and delivery. The story of the conference call system that announced a billing delinquency to everyone on the call . . . well, you'll just have to read it.

Change is hard, but Eric and Mike aren't advocating wholesale change overnight. They point out plenty of places to start, including some changes that are simply matters of framing, not painful business-process surgeries. The completion of a task—like an order confirmation—can become a word-of-mouth victory when it becomes part of an experience. I've already shared the glory of the CD Baby follow-up email (Chapter 9) with others, and I'm not even a customer.

The funnel treated customers as outputs of a linear process. In an era when trust in traditional sources has eroded—in government, media, and in companies and the marketing they employ—word-of-mouth from trusted peers serves as input into both returning and new business.

Here are stories worth sharing and learning from.

BRIAN HALLIGAN
Cofounder and CEO of HubSpot

A PRACTICAL STORY OF DIGITAL TRANSFORMATION

We get it. The content and ideas in this book are sometimes challenging to apply in real businesses. "How would I make this work in my company?" is a question we hear all the time.

There are a lot of moving parts and metrics, a lot of tactics and tools, and a lot of execution. Change is hard, and what we're proposing here requires a number of changes across a number of teams and departments.

The purpose of our fable (located in between chapters, starting after chapter two) is to make it feel a little easier; to provide some practical and conversational insights into how you can overcome concerns and fears; and to show you how to apply some of these ideas today, in order to see real change tomorrow.

We hope it helps.

R.I.P. THE SALES FUNNEL: 1898–2018. "IT HAD A GOOD RUN."

People love to buy; they don't like to be sold.
—JIM CATHCART, *RELATIONSHIP SELLING*

Lee Iacocca, the man responsible for bringing Chrysler back from the brink in the 1980s, wrote in his autobiography that when he first assumed the helm,

> At regular intervals the Manufacturing Division would tell the Sales Division how many and what types of vehicles they were going to produce. Then it

would be up to the Sales Division to try to sell them. This was completely ass backwards in my book.[1]

We couldn't have said it better ourselves, Lee.

Sitting here in the twenty-first century, such an approach to business seems absurd. You manufacture whatever you want, then expect the sales department to sell it all? No wonder car salesmen always seem so pushy! No wonder dealerships used to have "fire sales" where they practically gave cars away. No wonder Chrysler teetered on the verge of bankruptcy.

In the automotive industry's infancy, mass-produced, commercially available cars were such a revolutionary step forward that the global market had a voracious appetite for the then-disruptive technology. The demand was so vast that it didn't matter what the manufacturer produced: people bought. Factories couldn't churn cars out fast enough. Manufacturers didn't need to be responsive to what customers wanted because demand far outstripped supply. This reality led to Henry Ford's famous quip "A customer can have a car painted any color he wants as long as it is black." Today, we look back at such statements and think, *How shortsighted! How arrogant!* But regardless what color consumers preferred, they still bought as many black Model Ts as Henry Ford could produce.

Operating from that paradigm, no wonder Chrysler

---

1   Lee Iacocca, *Iacocca: An Autobiography* (New York: Bantam Books, 1986).

2

made as many cars as it wanted, however it wanted. The company came from a world where the suppliers held all the power. It had the resources, the capital, and the assets to feed a seemingly endless demand. But when the market began to slow, Chrysler somehow missed the memo. It kept charging forward the way it had for decades. Finally, management realized something was wrong and brought in Iacocca to turn things around.

Chrysler lived in a world of dominance until it faced the reality of desperation.

Information Then and Now: From Oasis to Ocean

What happened to the car industry has happened to every industry's sales and marketing departments. There was a time when salespeople drove the sales process. The marketing people delivered the message and made prospects aware of what the company sold to get them in the proverbial door. Then the salespeople took over and dragged the prospect over the finish line, whether they wanted to go or not. Faced with few options, the buyer either went along or dropped out altogether . . . only to face the same situation when they took their business next door.

That's no longer the reality we live in. Thanks to technology and the global economy, buyers have more options than ever. But more importantly, they have access to more information about their options.

They don't need to come to you. They don't need to call your sales department. They don't need to come to your showroom. They don't need to get someone on the phone to explain the pros and cons of on-premises servers versus cloud servers. They don't need to go to the library to figure out if this food is healthy or not. They don't have to call every store in town to see if someone has a certain part available. They don't have to leave their home or office—or even pick up the phone—to find an ultra-specific specialty item and have it delivered straight to their doorstep. The barriers to entry in virtually every industry have fallen. Where before consumers were beholden to companies to produce the goods and services they needed, there's now a surplus of providers. Global shipping, innovations in logistics, and the Internet have worked together so that, in the words of Thomas Friedman, "the world is flat." Consumers have more choices than ever before. Regardless of what products or services you sell, you face intense competition. Local artisans face direct competition from other artisans on Etsy or eBay half a continent away. Regional manufacturers have to compete on price against low-cost manufacturers half a world away. Global financial institutions now go toe-to-toe with online companies without a brick-and-mortar branch and just a click away.

Obviously, companies no longer hold the power.

No one in business today can imagine trying to run a company as Chrysler or Ford did, much less believe they could succeed. The paradigm has shifted. Our customers don't need us. Alternatives, expert opinions, third-party validation, transparent user reviews—it's all out there on the Internet for the entire world to see. We are no longer the gatekeepers of vital information for decision-making. Quite the opposite: the floodgates have burst wide open.

Consumers don't need information; they're drowning in it.

The Sales Funnel Belongs in a Museum (with Other Antiques)

From this now-outdated reality sprang the original sales funnel.

In fact, the traditional funnel goes back at least as far as 1898 and perhaps even earlier than that. It was created in the context of consumers who had limited options, an abundance of attention, and a dependence on the purveyors of products and services they needed to help them make a decision.

Does that sound like your daily life? Didn't think so.

The old sales funnel worked on the AIDA model: attention, interest, desire, and action. Our attention is at a premium these days. Depending on how you measure it, the average American is exposed to hundreds or even thousands of messages a day. Consumers don't have attention to spare as they did in 1909.

When we have a problem, we don't call a salesperson first to help us figure out what we should do. We just pull out our phones and do a quick search. Entire services are dedicated to helping you manage all the emails, texts, and other messages you receive on an hourly basis. The idea that attention is an abundant resource that you can fill with ads and see results simply doesn't work in this new world.

Here's another one of the sales funnel's fatal flaws: it's from the company's point of view. That made sense back in the day when consumers were unwary sheep, ripe for the shearing (as many companies saw them—cue a random scene from *Mad Men*). That's no longer reality. When was the last time you tried a new restaurant without checking it out online first? We don't know about you, but we like *not* being a restaurant's guinea pigs, walking in the front door while wondering if it's going to be a hit or a miss. When was the last time someone contacted your company without trying to Google their problem first? When was the last time one of your salespeople spoke to a genuine prospect who knew next to nothing about what you sold? We've gone so far the other way that millions of people now diagnose their medical problems at home and just come to the doctor to get a prescription—by name!

The funnel doesn't work in a world where people don't need to go through you to find the facts they need to make a decision. Despite that fact, most marketing models still begin with "awareness," as in, is the prospect aware of the company? (See how that question doesn't start from the customer's perspective but from the company's: "Do they know about us?") Next usually comes "education." Not in the sense that the customer wants to learn something, but "what educational material can we push on them?" The sales funnel comes from the mentality of "we, the company, are in control. Now, what are *we* going to do *to* them?"

The sales funnel worked when it was a simpler time. People moved down a linear, gravity-fed process to the bottom of the funnel. Things tended to move in one direction: toward the sale. Reality is a bit more complex than that. How many of your own prospects have you seen take one step forward and two steps back? It happens all the time, yet the sales funnel doesn't reflect this common occurrence at all.

In *Fire Your Sales Team Today,* we sounded the death knell of sales as we knew it. Your salespeople can't operate independently of your marketing efforts. Not if you want to be successful in the twenty-first century.

Now, we're sounding the death knell of the sales funnel.

We started talking about killing the funnel in a blog article from February 14, 2018, titled "What Does Today's New Revenue Generation Funnel Look Like?" HubSpot started showing the following graphic (Figure 1A) in May, then doubled down on the idea that the funnel is dead in September at INBOUND 2018. They proposed it be replaced with what they call the flywheel (Figure 1B). While we believe the flywheel is a great start and captures the elements of the new buyer journey, we feel practitioners need something more detailed and action-oriented—something to pull in strategy, tactics, analytics, and technology. We need something that reflects this new reality—a world where buyers hold the power, where attention is at a premium, and where we're all faced with more information, misinformation, and disinformation than ever before.

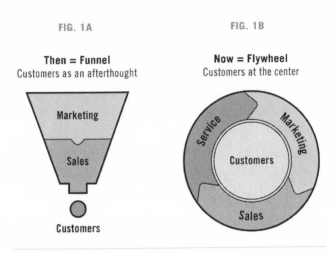

FIG. 1A

FIG. 1B

Then = Funnel
Customers as an afterthought

Marketing

Sales

Customers

Now = Flywheel
Customers at the center

Service

Marketing

Customers

Sales

How People Buy—Whether B2B or B2C

How has buying behavior changed?

On the retail front, consumers are shifting from brick-and-mortar to e-commerce. No surprise there; Amazon's Jeff Bezos is now the richest man in the world. Online retail accounted for more than nine percent of all

U.S. retail sales in 2017[2] and was projected to reach almost fourteen percent by 2021.[3]

What might come as a surprise, though, is that business-to-business sales (B2B) are following suit. At the end of 2017, tech research giant Forrester estimated that B2B e-commerce composed eleven percent of all B2B sales in the U.S.—note that that's more than business to consumer (B2C)—and forecasted it to reach more than thirteen percent by 2021, exceeding a trillion dollars.

It shouldn't come as a shock that people are doing more buying online, both for themselves and for their companies. The flip side of those numbers is that, despite all the hype about online sales, more than eighty-five percent of all B2C and B2B revenue still happens the good old-fashioned way.

Except it doesn't.

While the point of purchase may look the same (e.g., a cash register or a purchase order), the *way* the buyer arrived at that point looks vastly different:

- Forty-four percent of people start product

---

2   U.S. Bureau of the Census, "E-Commerce Retail Sales as a Percent of Total Sales (ECOMPCTSA)," Federal Reserve Economic Data, July 5, 2018, https://fred .stlouisfed.org/series/ECOMPCTSA.

3   Statista, "E-Commerce Share of Total Retail Sales in United States from 2013 to 2021," Statista, November 2017, https://www.statista.com /statistics/379112/e-commerce-share-of-retail-sales-in-us/.

searches with Amazon versus thirty-four percent using search engines.[4]

- Seventy-eight percent of local mobile searches result in an offline purchase.[5]

- Seventy-one percent of B2B shopping research starts with a generic search.[6]

- Seventy-two percent of B2B shoppers do twelve searches on average before engaging with a website even once.[7]

This minuscule sample of shopping data offers just a glimpse at how buying behavior has fundamentally changed. Depending on which report you read, your average B2B buyer is anywhere from half to two-thirds of the way through their decision-making process before they ever reach out to the suppliers they're looking at. How many sales opportunities have you lost without even knowing you were in the race? The path from wanting to buy something to arriving at a purchase has radically changed, thanks in large part to the digital revolution (more information) and globalization (more choices).

4   BloomReach, "State of Amazon 2016," BloomReach, 2016, http://go.bloomreach
    .com/rs/243-XLW-551/images/state-of-amazon-2016-report.pdf.

5   Neustar Inc., "Trends Shaping Local Search in 2014," Neustar, May 7, 2014,
    https://www.slideshare.net/NeustarInc/trends-shaping-local-search-in-2014.

6   Kelsey Snyder and Pashmeena Hilal, "The Changing Face of B2B Marketing,"
    Google, March 2015, https://www.thinkwithgoogle.com/consumer-insights
    /the-changing-face-b2b-marketing/.

7   Ibid.

Do you remember when you'd go to your local grocery store to buy some butter? A young friend of ours recently went shopping. Faced with nine different options, he froze. That was too much information to sort through. He actually left the grocery store without buying at all because he couldn't figure out what he was supposed to do. And that's just butter!

Even as late as the 1990s, the average grocery store carried less than seven thousand individual products. Today, that number has swollen to more than forty thousand in a single store. (Did you know there are twenty-two different kinds of Cheerios!?) In *The Paradox of Choice,* author Barry Schwartz breaks down the psychology of how consumers make decisions faced with an overwhelming amount of options. Often, they do exactly what our young friend did: they postpone the decision altogether. This holds true for most people, whether they're buying jam or selecting a mutual fund for their employee retirement account.

This isn't just the case for consumers; this is increasingly the reality for B2B decision-makers as well. Not too long ago a fairly clear delineation existed between consumer products and service versus those for business. We remember when Drexel University's engineering department got a desktop computer. It made the headlines in the local papers because it was such a big deal for university students to have access to a machine previously available only for big businesses and major labs. (We promise that we marketing students sneaking in to have a crack at it did far cooler stuff with it than those engineers did.) Coming at it from the other side, plenty of consumer products are now being used as business tools, like the work we're doing with Fitbit to sell their devices to health-care insurance companies as part of employee wellness programs. And remember when "serious" professionals only used Black-Berrys, scoffing at iPhones as "toys" for consumers? The previously clear line between B2C and B2B has blurred almost to the point of obscurity.

Not only do your potential customers face a vast array of options when deciding what to buy, but they also live in a deluge of influences and information surrounding these decisions. There is a staggering amount of content available on every conceivable (and inconceivable) topic, activity, product, service, and idea. How much? To give you a taste, here is how much content is uploaded, created, and distributed online *in a single minute*:[8]

- 500 hours of YouTube videos

- 3.3 million Facebook posts

- 1,440 WordPress posts

- 448,000 Tweets

- 29 million WhatsApp messages

- 149,513 emails

---

8   Robert Allen, "What Happens Online in 60 seconds?" Smart Insights, February 6, 2017, https://www.smartinsights.com/internet-marketing -statistics/happens-online-60-seconds/.

Every . . . sixty . . . seconds.

Think about your own life. How many ads do you hear on your way to work? How many online and offline articles do you see? How many different LinkedIn posts do you scroll through? How many emails do you get a day? How often does your phone ding with a new message or a notification? We all live in this crazy whirlwind of people and companies constantly vying for our attention, our trust, and our dollars.

A Whole New World = A Wholly Different Worldview

The sales funnel can't adequately capture how a buyer goes through their daily life. People get stuck at certain points. They're ready to make a decision, but then they go out to dinner with their brother-in-law, who says, "Oh no, don't do that! Let me tell you about a friend of mine—" and then they're back in the land of indecision.

Perhaps they usually buy cage-free eggs, but last night they saw an exposé on cage-free farms, and now they're unsure of which brand they can trust. Maybe they're ready to trade in their car for the new model, but now that they have a baby, they're more safety conscious, and so they look at crash statistics for the first time ever.

There is no neat, sequential process anymore. Trying to force an old perspective on this new reality doesn't work. A paradigmatic shift in buyer behavior requires a paradigmatic shift in how we look at buyer behavior and—more importantly for companies—a paradigmatic shift in how we align revenue generation with that behavior.

That's why we've smashed the funnel.

We can no longer afford to be company-centric: "How do we generate leads?" That treats buyers as commodities in a process. You might as well be asking, "How do we get more cattle into our slaughterhouse?" While we doubt that's how you think of your customers (or, at least, we hope it's not), by its very nature the sales funnel focuses on the company. We don't even like the metaphor of a sales pipeline because, again, it assumes customers are commodities to be pushed and pulled through the company's process. A company should be their customer's trusted personal companion in the buying journey.

We have to change the model and our mindsets to become customer-centric. Our questions have to change. How can we influence each person's decision-making process? How can we help them make the best decision for their unique context? How can we meet them where they are? How can we give them what they want, what they're looking for, and what they need? How can we help them through this whirlwind—this cyclone—of information, influences, and decisions that they face?

For the past twenty years, if not thirty, sales and marketing professionals have been trying to adapt the funnel to account for this paradigmatic shift. They're trying to project an outdated concept onto a reality that no longer even remotely aligns to it. It's time to lay the funnel aside. It's brought us this far. It's served us far longer than it should have. Continuing to cling to it doesn't just hinder your revenue efforts; it hurts them.

Today's buyer journey is more reflective of a cyclone, like the one in Figure 2—or a series of such cyclones. By shifting to thinking of your buyers in cyclones, you'll have a new perspective on how to influence them to move through each one, resulting in a bigger impact on your revenue.

FIG. 2

For many businesspeople, and especially marketers schooled in traditional thought and methods, this sounds like blasphemy. The business world has used the sales funnel as the underlying concept for nearly all marketing frameworks for generations now. It's withstood the test of time, with roots stretching back to the 1890s. It's been at the core of every serious sales and marketing plan in every major company of any size and note for over a century . . . which is really our point.

People don't buy like they used to. The world has moved on.

The sales funnel doesn't work in this reality where buyers now have the power. Buyers sit in the driver's seat, and unless you seriously stand out, they're going to speed past you like so many billboards on the highway. It doesn't matter how great you think you are because your opinion no longer matters. All that matters is what the buyer thinks of you—if they even think of you at all.

It did its job. It served its purpose. It's outlived its usefulness.

Let the funnel die in peace.

A WHISPER IN A CYCLONE: THE BUYER'S JOURNEY

No one can persuade another to change. Each of us guards a gate
of change that can only be opened from the inside. We cannot open
the gate of another, either by argument or by emotional appeal.

—MARILYN FERGUSON

"It's a twister! It's a twister!"

Who doesn't remember watching *The Wizard of Oz*
for the first time, fearing for Dorothy as she runs home
looking for Auntie Em, battling gusting winds and debris
all the while?

After she's knocked out and the tornado lifts the
house off the ground, she awakens in the midst of the

twister to all manner of strange things flying in front of her bedroom window: chickens squawking in their floating coop, Auntie Em contentedly knitting in her apparently magic rocking chair, and a cow calmly mooing as it flies through the air.

"We must be up inside the cyclone!" Dorothy shouts at Toto, just before Miss Gulch pedals by on her bicycle and turns into the Wicked Witch of the West riding on her broomstick.

Classic movie, but also a great analogy for understanding how and why people buy. This bizarre collection of scenes whirling around Dorothy happens to your buyer. Daily. We all live in a cyclone of information, facts, messages, communication, interactions, news, industry disruptions, global changes, and more. In the midst of all that, we're all trying to make the right decisions for everything we buy, from what we want for lunch to whether we should make a substantial investment in our business infrastructure this year or wait till next.

This book isn't about tactics. It's about helping you understand the true problem you face in revenue generation. Your competition isn't just your competitors; it's anything that deters a buyer from doing business with you. That's everything from choosing another provider to postponing a paralyzing decision all the way down to their love life and what mood they're in today. That's what you're up against: not just other providers but other influences, activities, and events completely unrelated to your company in any way. If you want to win at this game, you have to understand what game you're playing in the first place.

Avatars, Personas, and Shoppers—Who Buys!?

Forgive us if we're about to tell you something you already know. Unfortunately, we've seen so many companies fail to adequately perform this exercise that we can't assume you already have.

Who buys from you? Forget market demographics and data. Those can help point you in the right direction, but they're not the ultimate answer. You need to know more than simply their age and income—you need to get inside their head. Where are they in their life's journey? Are they part of the sandwich generation, providing for their aging parents as well as their struggling children? Do they identify more with their nationality or their ethnicity? Are they more likely to watch *Game of Thrones* or *NCIS*? Do they prefer the format of an e-book, audio book, or hard copy book? You can't answer those questions until you really know your buyer, and you don't know your buyer until you really know your current (or target) market.

We once worked with an original equipment manufacturer (OEM) supplying GM, Ford, and Chrysler that brought us in because they wanted to sell more of their widgets. The obvious course of action (to us, at least) was to build on their past success:

1. Sell more widgets to their existing clients by either offering more widget models for different car models or taking market share away from competing suppliers (as manufacturers usually have multiple suppliers of the same product).

2. Go after other carmakers or similar companies where their widgets would be bought wholesale; manufacturers in the maritime industry, for one, would have been an excellent secondary market.

In a roundtable with them, one of the company leaders suggested they go after do-it-yourselfers and sell their widgets via their website. While we applauded his willingness to look for answers in completely uncharted waters—and we wish more executives would follow in his footsteps—we then examined the idea's validity: "Well, let's look at these two different buyers. One is the OEM procurer for a carmaker who can place an order for a half-million sale every year. What's more, we can easily identify these people. For next to nothing, we can buy or build a list of their names and contact info. It's easy to reach that buyer; it just requires some smart tactics. On the other hand, there's the DIYer who doesn't know your company exists. Creating e-commerce functionality wouldn't be that difficult, but getting them to come to your site in the first place would be, not to mention all the new marketing assets we'd need to create to effectively sell to that guy in the first place and—"

Before we could even point out that once the DIYer fixed his car, he'd never need them again and therefore would provide zero customer lifetime value, the executive countered with, "Well, we can just advertise on NASCAR Sirius XM! That's all we'd have to do!"

This is a great example on two levels. One, it shows that the executive was headed in the right direction by putting himself in the buyer's shoes. A lot of weekend mechanics do, in fact, watch NASCAR and therefore probably enjoy its Sirius radio station. He was absolutely getting in the right mindset to sell to that buyer. At the broader level, though, it also puts into perspective the effort of selling to either of those avatars, not only from a sales and marketing perspective but from the viewpoint of operations, too.

We're not trying to ridicule the executive, but his line of thinking happens far too often. Instead of trying to get a more granular understanding of the current buyer and do a more effective job of reaching them, many company leaders look for easy answers (e.g., advertise more, sell to more types of customers, or "do something with that social media stuff").

We are far past the days of silver bullets and Magic 8 Balls. Sustainable, long-term revenue generation relies on a deep understanding of your buyer, from before they even know they need you all the way to dealing with them when they become irate.

But don't think that such a psychographic profile doesn't also apply to the cold logic of a fact-based B2B buyer:

In fact, exclusive research shown to Marketing Week finds that B2B brands fare better when they use emotive rather than rational marketing messages.

The study, conducted by CEB . . . in partnership with Google, suggests that although B2B buying is often treated as an activity influenced solely by logical factors such as cost-benefit analyses, risk assessments and feasibility studies, **in reality the process is determined by the same complex mix of gut instinct, emotion, reason** and post-rationalisation **that drives all human decisions.**[9]

The reporter in this *Marketing Week* article goes on to present the findings from a survey of three thousand B2B buyers and fifty B2B marketing organizations. The numbers are there: the more that B2B marketing looks like B2C, the more effective it is. So not only are the lines between the two blurring, but the more personalized your marketing message, the more effective it is, regardless of your industry.

After conducting a bit of in-depth research, a McKinsey data analysis concluded that

the research reinforced our belief in the importance not only of **aligning all elements of marketing**—strategy, spending, channel management, and message—with the journey that consumers undertake when they make purchasing decisions but also of integrating those elements across the organization. When marketers understand this journey and **direct their spending and messaging to the moments of maximum influence**, they stand a much greater chance of reaching consumers in the right place at the right time with the right message.[10]

Thank you, McKinsey. You took the words right out of our mouths.

The Eight Cyclones of the Buyer's Journey

We'd love to pretend that humans are rational, logical beings. We're not. Subsequently, any model that tries to find some kind of reasonable, sequential order in how we make decisions is going to fall short of reality. Our brains aren't wired to think like computers: ones and zeros, black and white, step one and step two. We're constantly amassing information, constantly changing, constantly reassessing.

That's why we see the buyer's mindset not as an orderly sequence of events but as a cyclone of motivations,

---

10   David Court, Dave Elzinga, Susan Mulder, and Ole Jorgen Vetvik, "The Consumer Decision Journey," McKinsey & Company, June 2009, https://www.mckinsey.com /business-functions/marketing-and-sales/our-insights/the-consumer-decision -journey; emphasis added.

rationalizations, and emotions. It's why we make impulse purchases that we regret (sometimes instantly) and why even the most analytical of financial wizards were completely blindsided by the Great Recession. We're just not that logical.

Here's a better way to think about and plan for the new buyer journey. We call it the Cyclonic Buyer Journey (Figure 3), covering the areas of marketing, sales, and customer service. You need all three to drive revenue in this new era.

Through a lot of field-tested techniques and research, we've identified eight key inflection points—the "moments of maximum influence," as McKinsey would say—where you have an opportunity to nudge your buyer's thinking. For the sake of explanation, we call them the eight cyclones. But we want to underscore that your buyer does not think in a straight line. The eight cyclones in Figure 3 help you visualize this new paradigm, but the reality is that there's just one massive whirlwind continually spinning around in their head. Their mindset might shift from one mentality (one cyclone) to another and skip the other ones we've laid out here. This isn't a left foot, right foot process. This is human psychology and psychology is messy.

The first thing you should notice is that this model does not center on you, the provider. Until the buyer finds themselves about halfway through their buying journey, you're a footnote in the process, at best.

FIG. 3

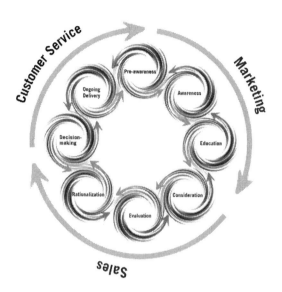

We've purposely labeled cyclones three through seven to reflect the reality that you don't sit in the driver's seat; the cyclones are named by the action the buyer is taking. The buyer is firmly behind the wheel; you're just along for the ride—if they let you in the car at all. The last cyclone (Delivery) is arguably the most important, as the buyer has to have a remarkable experience in order to become an advocate for your business. (See Table 1 to understand the nuances between the buyer's intent and mindset at each stage in the Cyclonic Buyer Journey.)

You're not educating them; they are self-educating. If you're smart, some of the material they use may be yours,

Cyclone	What the Buyer Thinks	How the Buyer Sees You	Responsible Departments
Pre-awareness	Unaware of existing or upcoming problem	They don't	Marketing and Sales
Awareness	There's a problem . . . but it's not enough to worry about	They don't	Marketing
Education	Actively searching for information on how to fix the problem	One of many provider options	Marketing
Consideration	Decided on path; looking at a variety of options	One of many	Marketing
Evaluation	Looking at a handful of potential providers	One of few	Marketing and Sales
Rationalization	Dotting i's and crossing t's, focusing on the details, covering their asses	Under a microscope	Sales
Decision-making	Ready to sign	Cautiously excited to get started	Sales
Ongoing Delivery	Depends on you (mostly)	Depends on you (mostly)	Customer Service

but plenty of it will come from other sources. You don't close the sale; they make the decision. This isn't about what you're doing to them but rather about the opportunity you have to influence their thinking.

Then, too, you also must be aware that your buyer isn't alone. There are always other parties who influence your buyer's choices. Regardless of whether your buyer has to take into account their oversight committee, a key employee, their significant other, the reactions of their close friends, or even a nagging parent's voice inside their head, your buyer *always* has someone else's opinion to consider before moving forward.

Strategy before tactics: that's been the mantra for ourselves, our other businesses, and our clients' businesses for years. Unfortunately, like the NASCAR Sirius XM idea, human nature looks for easy solutions—the magic bullet or the one key that's going to unlock everything else. Plenty of sales and marketing experts out there are more than happy to tell you (and sell you) their version of a cure-all: Case studies. Video. Retargeting. Account-based marketing. Rich-text email. Outbound sales. Inbound marketing. Social media engagement. Compounding blogs over decaying blogs. Companies keep pursuing these different tactics, trying to win battles even while losing the war.

Do you know what the number one problem professional marketers say they have? It's generating leads, of course. Everybody knows that. But what's their number two problem? Proving return on investment (ROI).[11] What's their number three problem? "Securing enough budget"... which they could solve if they could effectively address problem number two.

It's no wonder that when companies face falling revenue, one of the first places they cut is marketing. If you can't prove ROI, then everything you do is really just a crapshoot, isn't it? An astounding eighty percent of marketers admit that their lead generation activities are "only slightly or somewhat effective."[12]

We don't lay the blame entirely on marketing professionals. Much of the fault lies in the shortsightedness of company management. It's been our experience that plenty of company leaders want quick results. (Don't we all.) But this attitude puts pressure on marketers to do or look for things that promise immediate results. It puts pressure on the salespeople to engage in activities that promise quick returns. The problem is that today's buyers are more jaded, wary, and overwhelmed than ever before. The time-honored blue-light specials, "going out of business" sales, and other gimmicks aren't effective long-term strategies. They're not supposed to be. Revenue generation is about the long game:

11   HubSpot, "State of Inbound 2017," HubSpot, 2017, https://cdn2.hubspot .net/hubfs/53/assets/soi/2017/global/State%20of%20Inbound%202017 .pdf?t=1529949369593&__hstc=20629287.c7d35e684e957dd90b0623 31c03776a0.1464898340195.1529947084818.1529949375423.9& __hssc=20629287.4.1529949375423&__hsfp=3622431204.

12   BrightTALK, "B2B Lead Generation," BrightTALK, 2015, http://go.brighttalk.com /rs/105-RTY-982/images/Holger_B2B_Lead_Gen_Report.pdf.

long-term efforts and long-term payoff. You can't play the long game with a short-term mindset.

To win, you need a granular understanding of the opponent you're up against. It's not "the other guys," it's not the latest industry IPO (initial public offering), it's not the store across town. It's *everything*; you're up against everything. Too vague? How about we walk you through a scenario just about everyone outside of New York City can relate to.

Let's go buy a car.

A Buyer's Journey in Real Life

Your only child is going to be getting their driver's license soon, so you decide to pass your current commuter Camry down to them and finally go buy yourself something nice. Since you won't have to play chauffeur anymore, you want a sporty coupe. Should you go for a Lexus or a BMW? On your lunch break, you go online to do some comparison shopping.

In the traditional way of categorizing buyers, most marketers would put you in the awareness or maybe education phase because you're gathering information to make a buying decision. The way we define it, you're in the Evaluation cyclone. You could have solved your dilemma by buying your child a used car instead of passing down yours and buying a new one. You skipped past all the makes and models of automobiles you could buy. In your head, you're just trying to decide whether you want a Lexus or a BMW.

Later that evening, when you mention this to your frugal spouse, they say, "I thought we agreed that we were going to downsize." Well, yes, you argue, a two-seater is certainly smaller than a sedan. They respond with, "I thought 'downsize' meant 'less expensive.'"

Now you feel bad. While you could already imagine that new car smell, they were worrying about paying for your kid's college in a couple of years. You sigh and silently shelve your lifelong dream of a red sports car for a few more years. Okay, you'll settle for something more financially prudent. While waiting for your food curbside that night, you whip out your phone and start looking at all the latest makes and models from the major manufacturers.

With this external influence (your spouse's frowning frugality), you've gone backward from a mindset of Evaluation to one of Consideration. Instead of comparing two specific cars, you're in the market for a new car in general.

The next day at work, you start hearing rumors that the company might be in trouble. You try to ignore them because it usually turns out to be nothing. Still, though . . .

That evening, your spouse says, "I crunched the numbers. This is how much we need to be saving every month for college." You nearly have a heart attack—has tuition really gone up that much!? And if the company really *is* in trouble . . .

It's too risky. Your kid won't get their license for a few

months, and they're not expecting a car until their birthday a few months after that anyway. You decide your Camry is getting you back and forth to work just fine and shelve the whole idea of getting another car for now.

With these two new pieces of information, you're no longer even in the Consideration phase. You've spun around the cyclone to wind up back in the mindset of Awareness. Yes, you want your kid to have a car, but there isn't a pressing need to do anything about it right now.

Fast-forward a few months. The rumors turned out to be true. You managed to hang on to your job, but there were plenty of people let go, and things are still quite uncertain. At this rate, you're not even sure you want a new car note hanging over your head. Maybe you should just buy yourself a used car that's great on gas mileage for your commute. Or maybe you need to let go of the idea of getting a third car altogether. Your kid's only sixteen and *your* parents didn't buy you a car at that age.

Here, you're in the Education mindset. Instead of firmly deciding on a course of action (buying a new car), you're now thinking about other ways to solve your issue—including forgoing a purchase altogether.

After talking it over with your spouse and knowing that you don't want to renege on a promise, the two of you decide to buy your kid a decent used car, paying half from your savings and financing the rest. But you've never bought a used car before. How do you make sure you don't get taken for a ride? Should you buy from a dealership? Is it cheaper to buy from a used car lot? You'd feel okay buying a cheaper car if you knew your kid was going to start at the local community college, but what if they get a scholarship to go out of state? You'd definitely want something more reliable if they'll be living farther away.

Once again, you find yourself in a Consideration mindset: you know you're going to buy a used car, but there are so many new things to factor into your decision now.

After a few weeks of online searching, you decide CarMax is the best option. You don't have to haggle, they have a nationwide inventory, and they provide so many guarantees that it just makes you feel secure, regardless of which car you pick.

You show up at the lot (for the first time, by the way) with your spouse and teenager to test drive a couple of cars that the three of you picked out online the night before, and your kid falls in love with a crossover that looks like it belongs in a car commercial featuring a bunch of teenagers at the beach. Everything's great.

You're in the Decision-making mindset. The decision has been made; all you need to do is sign the papers.

While waiting for the sales rep to put together said paperwork, you idly Google the stats on the cute crossover and find that it has a long history of defects. Whoa! Car repair costs and the possibility of your kid being stranded on the side of the road in another state—that's the last thing you want! Maybe you need to rethink this before you sign those papers . . .

The Crux of This Book: Why We Buy (or Not)

Do you see how even with something as commonplace as buying a car, a person's decision-making can ping-pong back and forth? That's what we mean by "cyclone." These external factors that the car dealerships had no control over (or even knowledge of) took their prospective customer around and around, from getting ready to buy a BMW coupe to postponing a decision to winding up keeping their car and buying the kid another one altogether . . . again, all without the other dealerships even knowing they were in the race.

It doesn't matter what you sell: software or hardware, consumer goods or professional services, health care or home care—Dorothy's bizarre cyclone mirrors the mental whirlwind your buyer goes through. There's not an orderly, sequential funnel for them to follow. There's no path to walk or maze to be solved.

That's why tactics matter far less than a basic understanding of buying psychology. Once you understand your buyer's journey and identify the key points of influence, you'll have an overall strategy that will work, regardless of which tools or media you use to execute that strategy.

Starting with the next chapter, we're going to go in depth on all eight cyclones, including the three different experiences your buyer will have in the cyclone of Delivery. This book isn't meant to be prescriptive. We've included an appendix of tools, tactics, and metrics to help you navigate your own whirlwind, but the goal of this book is to help you completely reframe your perspective on marketing, sales, and overall revenue generation.

We've tried to cover as wide a variety of industries, examples, experiences, and hypotheticals as we can, not to prescribe a solution to your revenue woes but to inspire your thinking about how you see your buyer and how to influence them on their journey.

This book isn't about the answers but helping you ask better questions.

THUNDERBOLT IT

Julie Stern was at a personal crossroads.

Her IT consulting and staff augmentation firm, Thunderbolt IT, had not experienced growth for the past two years. Once again, she expected to end this year at around $45 million. She felt tired and frustrated. Though she once had grand plans for growing her company to $100 million and then selling it, this dream of a liquidity event seemed less likely with each passing year. She often wondered if she should give up on her goal or keep trudging along. Any way you sliced it, she was stuck.

Two clients, Greenway Bank and Genesis Financial Services, took up more of her personal time than was necessary. When she landed their business three years ago, it finally put her in the big leagues. Combined, the two companies accounted for around forty-five percent of Thunderbolt's revenue. Julie felt it was her number one responsibility to provide these clients with the utmost attention. Losing either of them would surely damage her business, and the prospect of that kept her awake at night.

Over the course of the last eighteen months, Julie had attempted to diversify her client base by building a new sales and marketing team—to generate sales leads, attract new opportunities, and close new clients faster and more frequently. She just finalized hiring Bonnie McAllister, her very first chief marketing officer, scheduled to start two weeks from Monday. She was excited and nervous at the same time.

I hope this works, she thought to herself.

There was only one problem with her plan. Julie's focus had always been on the operations side of the business—solving difficult technical problems. She was a thought leader in the IT industry and knew enough about sales and marketing to make it work. But over the past few years, both of these areas had changed so much that she was no longer sure she knew what she needed to know to grow—thus the new hire.

New clients had always come through networking and referrals; she had never needed a pipeline of leads before. It was becoming more and more obvious to her that her lack of knowledge was becoming an issue. "Hire smart people and let them do their jobs"—that's what the experts said.

She felt overwhelmed by all the dramatic changes going on in marketing: social media, paid digital ads, websites, and search—even marketing automation technology was a little intimidating. When she had time (which wasn't often), she would read some content online and watch some videos posted on LinkedIn. She even attended a marketing conference a few years back and read a book on marketing during her last vacation. Still, she didn't have a clear idea of how to build a consistent, repeatable, scalable, and predictable sales and marketing engine at Thunderbolt IT.

Seeking help, she decided to present this critical issue to her peer-to-peer CEO group. She'd been an active member of the group for six years and had always benefited from the other CEOs' counsel. They were like her advisory board, and they often shared diverse experiences, benefiting all the members. But as an introvert, she sometimes found it challenging to ask for help when it came to her own business issues. To psych herself up, she composed a brief summary of her challenges to present to the group at her next meeting on Tuesday. She titled it "A Question of Growth—A Strategy Crossroads for Thunderbolt IT."

The group listened carefully and asked thoughtful questions. Their consensus was unanimous: Thunderbolt IT did not have a strategy problem—it had a sales and marketing challenge. Everyone agreed that a great sales team and a consistent flow of qualified prospects could help her achieve her dream of creating a $100 million company.

One of the group members recommended she talk to Sam Roberts. Sam had recently sold his well-respected marketing firm to a larger agency and was looking for his next project. *Maybe he could mentor me?* she thought. She knew him from many years ago, when they were in a different networking group together. She was always impressed by his marketing presentations and his knack for explaining industry issues in easy-to-understand terms. He was at least ten years older than her but somehow seemed on top of all the latest sales and marketing trends.

She decided to send him a message on LinkedIn. To her delight, he suggested they meet and have coffee Thursday morning. He asked her to bring her sales and marketing reports.

On Wednesday morning, to prepare for that meeting, Julie asked her VP of sales, Jonathan Forstein, to send her a report showing what was currently in the pipeline. Jonathan replied that he didn't have a standard format to track sales opportunities but attached his personal spreadsheet with some notes. It had five columns:

Name of prospective company	Contact person	Amount of opportunity	Date of last follow-up call	Salesperson assigned to the account

Julie was pleased to see there were over sixty names on the list. She printed two clean copies to share with Sam and went to bed that night feeling optimistic.

Early the next morning at the Bean Café, they grabbed two coffees and got right down to business. Sam asked Julie to paint a picture of what she envisioned Thunderbolt

IT would look like when it reached its full potential. He told her to forget about budget and just "blue-sky it."

Julie told him she imagined hitting quarterly revenue targets and creating the new offerings that she always wanted to develop but had never found the time for. She envisioned a waiting list of smart candidates who were eager to join her firm. She and her management team would work on strategic initiatives and spend time innovating on the basic challenges her clients had in common. After a few years, she'd sell the company and move on to a more leisurely lifestyle: part consulting, part travel. Maybe she'd even take up rock climbing, she joked.

Sam laughed and agreed that this was a wonderful vision. He turned to the stack of printed spreadsheets and said, "Okay, now let's look at the numbers."

They both picked up their packets and spent a few minutes reading. When Sam was done, he asked Julie if she had anything else she wanted to share: "How do you manage the business, in general? What's your leadership style? How do you know if your employees are achieving their goals and objectives?"

Julie remembered her boss at her first job out of college, a real micromanager. She told Sam that she had sworn to herself, "If I ever start my own company, I will hire smart people and let them do their thing." This was her philosophy, and it had brought her to where they were today.

"Julie," he said, "you have built a great company and have a good shot at fulfilling your vision of what

Thunderbolt IT can be. But your company is sick—not gravely ill, but sick nonetheless—and it does have the potential of being in real danger if you lose just one of your two mammoth clients. It could cripple you so badly that it would take years to recover. Let's try to prevent that from happening."

Julie already knew this, but hearing Sam say it made her feel even more concerned.

"Luckily," he continued, "I have seen this exact scenario countless times in my career, and I have the cure."

Sam explained that Julie needed to understand how dramatically buyer behavior had changed, and that companies like hers were still executing marketing plans from 1995, when the world was a different place.

"There is so much noise out there today—cell phones pinging, Internet chatter, social media posts, advice from friends and family, and seven hundred cable channels, just to name a few sources of distraction. To your buyers, or even to me and you, doesn't it feel like we're in a cyclone when we try to buy anything these days?" he asked.

Julie agreed. She'd been getting tons of unsolicited emails, her LinkedIn feed was filled with crap, and everyone always had some bit of advice for her. It could be overwhelming at times.

For Thunderbolt IT's prospects, Sam reminded her, buying $250,000 to $500,000 worth of IT services was a very scary proposition. And if her target audience of CIOs didn't feel safe, they were not going to buy anything. People didn't make purchase decisions until they felt safe.

Sam went on to explain how Thunderbolt IT needed to create a buyer journey experience that strategically and tactically helped Julie's prospects feel safe. They needed lots of educational material, delivered in context to their buyer journey stage and their specific challenges. They needed to understand exactly which options were available and why Thunderbolt IT was the obvious choice to help them. Essentially, they needed to be guided through their buyer journey—their cyclones—and Thunderbolt's new marketing and sales processes would do just that.

"You've got to diversify your base of business and add solid clients to help propel your revenue," he said. "But Julie Stern can't be the lynchpin that holds this whole process together. You need to help your new CMO do the things necessary to build this new revenue generation program."

Julie admitted that she had a hard time understanding everything that would be required in order to do what Sam was suggesting. It would take change, investment, and new ways of thinking about sales and marketing. He said he could relate: in the run-up to selling his own business, he'd faced similar challenges.

He offered to mentor her through this important transition but said that all his advice would be useless . . . unless she could commit to three conditions:

1. She'd meet at the Bean Café every Thursday.

2. She'd follow Sam's advice to a T and agree to give it a fair shot—no matter how uncomfortable she was or how impatient she became.

3. She would not even think about changing priorities until they met their revenue goals for four consecutive quarters, because this was the most important work to be done at the company for the foreseeable future.

Julie's head was spinning. She had hoped that Sam would give her a few nuggets, not volunteer himself as a weekly accountability coach. She was overjoyed that a colleague she respected was confident in her vision for Thunderbolt IT, but she was nervous about committing to work with him. She knew very little about how sales and marketing were supposed to work today. The technology, the tactics, and the analytics were all new; what he was offering felt like a giant blind leap.

"I'm so grateful for your offer," she finally answered. And she truly was, *but* . . . "Can I take a day to consider your plan?"

"Of course," Sam said, "but every day that passes is one day further from accomplishing your goals."

She laughed and said she would get in touch soon.

It was 10:00 a.m. by the time she got back to her desk. Emails were already piling up in her inbox. Greenway Bank wanted a face-to-face that afternoon to discuss lagging results from their ongoing cloud migration project.

Genesis Financial Services wanted her to replace a recent software designer placement with a new contractor—at no charge, of course.

She stared at the laptop screen for ten minutes, daydreaming about what the company would look like when they got past that stage. She opened up a new email and selected Sam Roberts's name from her address book:

Sam,

I'm in. I agree to your three conditions. See you next Thursday at 7:00 a.m. at the Bean Café.

Best,
Julie

3

"DID YOU KNOW?": THE CYCLONE OF PRE-AWARENESS

If I'd listened to customers, I'd have given them a faster horse.

—HENRY FORD (APOCRYPHAL)

"I wish I'd known about this a month ago!"

Whatever your product or service, that is not something you want to hear from your target market, yet that is exactly what the founders of Updater heard time and again from their users.

Think back to the last time you moved. Think of the million and one tasks you had and all the details you had to keep track of. Forget the actual task of packing boxes, then loading and unloading the truck. Plenty of people hate that aspect of it, and they'll gladly pay a moving service to do it for them.

But what about transferring the power bill? What about forwarding your mail and updating your magazine subscriptions? What about canceling your newspaper delivery? Which telecom providers serve your new address, and how do you choose between them? Where do you go to find out who provides recycling services? If you're moving into an apartment, what about renter's insurance? If you're moving to a new state, what about registering your car? What about forgetting to register to vote until it's too late and missing out on the democratic process? And that's just the tip of the iceberg!

That's where Updater comes in.

The Perfect Solution to a Past Problem

Updater's app tracks all of these details for you. The problem the tech startup had was that its target users didn't realize how overwhelming moving is (or forgot from the last time). It wasn't until just a few days before the actual move that they started to panic and finally thought, *I wonder if there's an app for that?*

By the time they found Updater, there was still plenty to be done—and plenty they had overlooked entirely—but they had missed out on most of the value they could have enjoyed if they'd found the app even just a couple of weeks earlier. As a result, the company was losing out on most of the opportunities and great user experiences it could have had.

To solve this problem, Updater could have gone the traditional route and tried to reach people by, say, advertising. It could have bought Google ads for people searching for "moving companies" or "U-Haul." But that route came with two problems. One, they would be competing in an already overcrowded marketplace where thousands upon thousands of companies spend millions of advertising dollars, including the ultracompetitive real estate industry.

Two, trying to target Google searches like these addresses only a fraction of Updater's potential market. According to the U.S. Census, upward of thirty-five million people move in a given year. Of those, about twenty-three million stay within the same county. Isn't it conceivable that a few million of those might not hire a moving truck but bum a friend's pickup instead? They wouldn't Google "movers," "moving truck," or anything else that would result in being exposed to a relevant search ad.

The same census data also shows that another million movers relocated to a whole other country. How many hundreds of thousands of those individuals stored their belongings stateside and shipped the rest by freight? They certainly wouldn't search Google for their local U-Haul dealership. How many thousands of movers were relocated by their employers, whose human resources department arranged everything from the sale of their house to the moving and the unpacking? None of these numbers even take into account the half-million or so people officially moving into the United States every year, for whom the app might be invaluable if they've never lived stateside before.

By the time Updater's users began searching for help, it was almost too late.

They Had a Problem Long Before You Came Along

Any professional marketer will tell you that the sales process begins with a prospect in some type of pain. That pain can be anything from a problem they want to fix all the way to an emotional desire they want fulfilled. Absent that pain, your buyer will never take action. That's why mass advertising often has the two-fold purpose of trying to reach people experiencing that pain as well as increasing brand awareness so that when other people experience pain, the advertiser is the first brand they'll think of.

If Updater had clung to that conventional mindset, the company would be faced with either accepting incremental, organic growth or spending a small fortune on advertising in the hope that when someone did get ready to move, some part of their mind would go, *Hey, didn't I see an advertisement for something to help with moving?*

Neither seemed appealing.

Instead, Updater made a brilliant strategic move: it stopped marketing to its users and began marketing to real estate companies, moving companies, property management companies, universities, and others who had direct relationships with the exact people the company wanted to reach. It partnered with these organizations to create customized portals and checklists for the partners' movers so that the app was tailored exactly to what the movers needed. This strategy allowed those partners to foster communication, loyalty, and a higher image with their respective clients; gave the movers themselves a rich experience that made their lives far easier; and turned Updater into a B2B company that no longer had to worry about individual users finding them too late. Two years after the shift, the company saw 1,300 percent growth and users engaging with the app, on average, three to ten weeks ahead of their move.

Getting inside their buyer's head redefined their entire business.

Ignorance Is Bliss . . . for Those Who Reach a Buyer There

Updater found an elegant solution to what some professionals would call an impossible problem: how do you get someone to buy something they don't even know they need?

Previously, their users fell into the same kind of ill-prepared, ill-equipped mindset we all do from time to time. It's the seventy-six percent of us in the U.S. still buying Christmas gifts right up till December 25. It's why we often buy Valentine's Day presents on February 14 or buy a gift on the way to a party we RSVP'd to months ago. Plenty of businesses have meetings as a backhanded way to spur productivity, and nearly all of us have written a school paper the night before it was due. We know that these events are coming, but somehow we ignore them until just days or even hours before, then we say, "Holy %@*&! I'm not ready!"

This is what Updater's users experienced. Just days before the move, they would be suddenly struck by the realization that there were a million things to do, but they had no checklist to help them sort through it all. They would pull out their phone, Google "moving checklist," and stumble across Updater. In their decision-making process, they jumped from the Pre-awareness cyclone to Evaluation to Decision-making in just a matter of minutes. The opportunity for Updater to influence them in their buying journey was a small window.

But their time spent in Pre-awareness—not knowing that this "holy %@*&!" moment was coming down the pike—was a matter of weeks, if not months. What a huge window of opportunity . . . if only the company could figure out a way to reach their would-be users there!

That's the cyclone of Pre-awareness. The buyer's pain is coming. In fact, they may already have a problem they're unaware of. This is perhaps the most difficult of all cyclones in which to influence your buyer, but if you can, there is a wealth of opportunity. Perhaps in part because of Updater's success, there are now other moving apps vying for the same users. But because the company found the solution they did, Updater's users are presented with the solution before they even experience their problem, completely bypassing any would-be competitors. They move smoothly from Pre-awareness straight into Delivery because it's provided for them *gratis* by their real estate agent, moving company, university, or relocating service.

We freely admit that in some industries or for some products and services, it's much harder to identify buyers in the Pre-awareness cyclone. How can you possibly know that this is the year an old-school manufacturer will finally address the feedback from its sales team and decide it's time to invest in a customer relationship management (CRM) system? Companies make purchasing decisions for a huge variety of reasons. It could be as simple as one CEO feeling like she's falling behind after talking to another; once back at the office, she kicks her team in the butt, and the purchase is approved. How can you know which of those sales teams will suddenly be looking for sales enablement tech?

In some cases, it's almost impossible. A 2016 study published in the *New England Journal of Medicine* found that nearly half of all pregnancies in the United States are either mistimed (a woman wanted to conceive at some point but not at the time the pregnancy occurred) or unwanted (the woman did not want to ever conceive). If you provide obstetric care, how can you possibly predict when a woman will need your services?

In other industries, finding buyers in the Pre-awareness cyclone is easier. Staying on the topic of pregnancy, if you've had a child born in the United States in the last decade or so, you've inevitably received offers for child life insurance from Gerber. Understandably, few even want to consider the possibility of needing it. But did you know the United States has the highest child mortality rate out of the top twenty Organisation for Economic Co-operation and Development member countries?[13] It's an awful fact but true nonetheless. By the time someone needs such insurance for their child, it's already too late. Virtually the *only* time you can influence them to buy life insurance is in the Pre-awareness cyclone.

Or go back to the buyer cyclone example of buying a car from chapter two. If you know someone has a child and that they have a certain minimum income, you can statistically predict the likelihood that they'll be in the market for a new car within the next several months. Instead of waiting for them to walk into the dealership—and the data shows that the average buyer walks into only 1.7 dealerships before making a purchase—why not start influencing them in the Pre-awareness cyclone beforehand?

Better yet, why not start influencing the teenager instead? You can bet that in their buying journey (even

13   Organisation for Economic Co-operation and Development Health Data, "Infant Mortality Rates and International Rankings: Organisation for Economic Co-operation and Development (OECD) Countries, Selected Years 1960–2008," Centers for Disease Control, 2011, https://www.cdc.gov/nchs/data/hus/2011/020.pdf.

if mommy or daddy is the one footing the bill), they are already well past being aware of their upcoming pain. If you can influence them, they will, in turn, influence the actual buyer. It'd be smart to find the social media platform du jour for the children of affluent adults and then target some slick videos at fifteen- to eighteen-year-old users.

The McKinsey study we referenced in chapter two had this to say about carmakers:

> Companies like Chrysler and GM have long focused on using strong sales incentives and in-dealer programs to win during the active evaluation and moment-of-purchase phases. **These companies have been fighting the wrong battle**: the real challenges for them are the initial-consideration and post-purchase phases, which Asian brands such as Toyota Motor and Honda dominate with their brand strength and product quality. Positive experiences with Asian vehicles have made purchasers loyal to them, and that in turn generates positive word-of-mouth that increases the likelihood of their making it into the initial-consideration set. **Not even constant sales incentives by US manufacturers can overcome this virtuous cycle.**[14]

These companies win the fight before it even begins.

---

[14] David Court, Dave Elzinga, Susan Mulder, and Ole Jorgen Vetvik, "The Consumer Decision Journey," McKinsey & Company, June 2009, https://www.mckinsey.com/business-functions/marketing-and-sales/our-insights/the-consumer-decision-journey; emphasis added.

The Answer to a Problem They Didn't Know They Had

A great example of target-messaging people in the Pre-awareness stage comes from a cybersecurity client of ours. Chief information officers, chief technology officers, directors of technology and infrastructure, chief security officers, engineers, analysts, and administrators responsible for keeping their companies safe from cyber threats hope they are doing everything they can to protect their IT infrastructure. Unfortunately, Yahoo, Target, Chili's, Uber, Sony, Equifax, and others all thought they were secure only to find themselves the victims of massive hacks.[15] Reaching these people and their colleagues with an on-point message about better cybersecurity shouldn't be hard to do: "Bad guys could already be inside your network . . . and you don't even know it."

Such an ad would strike at an existing and ongoing fear that's so prevalent in their daily life that it should instantly evoke a "Hey, I should check this out" response. When they click on our client's ad that's similar, it takes them to a free offer to scan their network for existing breaches and latent intrusions where the hacker might be establishing a digital beachhead before launching a full-scale assault. Any engineer or chief information officer in their right mind would want to know if they had already fallen victim to such an attack without even realizing it.

---

15 Taylor Armerding, "The 17 Biggest Data Breaches of the 21st Century," CSO Online, January 26, 2018, https://www.csoonline.com/article/2130877 /data-breach/the-biggest-data-breaches-of-the-21st-century.

Pre-awareness tactics are particularly important with disruptive innovation. A *Harvard Business Review* article once said,

> Customers only know what they have experienced. They cannot imagine what they don't know about emergent technologies, new materials, and the like. What customer, for example, would have asked for the microwave oven, Velcro, or Post-It Notes? At the time the transistor was being developed, radio and television manufacturers were still requesting improved vacuum tubes.[16]

When reaching people in their Pre-awareness cyclone, the focus of your message shouldn't be about the revolutionary new gizmo, app, or process you have. They don't care about you. When you turn the attention on them to show them how it solves a problem they weren't even aware could be solved, that's when they sit up and start paying you that most valuable of all currencies: attention.

---

16 Anthony W. Ulwick, "Turn Customer Input into Innovation," *Harvard Business Review*, January 2002, https://hbr.org/2002/01/turn-customer-input-into-innovation.

THUNDERBOLT IT

They met at the Bean Café again on Thursday.

"How are you feeling?"

"Nervous, but optimistic!" Julie said.

Sam began that week's conversation by talking about the buyer journey and the stages people go through when they make a purchase. "Regardless of the purchase, people work though a decision-making process that ends up creating a buyer journey for them. The key to revenue growth is understanding your prospects' buyer journeys and mapping marketing, sales, and service to those stages."

Sam talked about how most people still considered the process to be a funnel, where prospects came in at the top and fell out of the bottom as customers. "That assumes that there is some kind of gravity pulling these people down toward a decision, which is no longer true. Today, most of the people you're marketing or selling to are in chaos; they are confused; they are inundated with content, opinions, and perspectives. It's more of a cyclone, a whirlwind, than a funnel."

He explained how most companies like Julie's were "late to the game," focusing their marketing on people who were ready to buy, instead of focusing it on people who were early in their buyer journey. He reminded her that more than ninety percent of the people looking for IT services were not ready to talk to a company yet—and that most marketers focused only on the ten percent who were. He encouraged Julie to focus on both. "Most are marketing to companies too late into the buying cycle and missing opportunities. The key is to get into a conversation early, so that your prospects can understand that they have serious challenges—maybe some they don't even realize they have. By being their guide early in the process, it positions Thunderbolt as a potential resource for education—and, hopefully, as a trusted advisor for when they're ready to talk to someone," Sam explained.

He asked Julie to talk with three people as she started her high-level research about her prospects' and customers' journeys: two of her existing clients and one prospect who never closed. "Ask them what they experienced in their buying journey prior to their first communication with Thunderbolt," he advised. "Listen to them talk about their experience, and see if it sounds cyclonic."

Over the next week, Julie arranged for three conference calls. She selected—

- Eric Michaels, a client who used most of Thunderbolt IT's services and had been a client for over a year

- Abby Franklin, a new client who was currently using their staff augmentation services—and who'd been discussing adding more services with the sales team

- Jeremy Mando, a prospective client with a large engagement, whom Thunderbolt IT had lost to a low-cost competitor

In her conversations with them, Julie was disappointed to hear that both of her clients—and the prospect—experienced exactly what Sam had described. Eric explained how he was so confused that he'd simply selected Thunderbolt IT because they were a local company and he knew they'd been in business for years. Abby didn't see much of a difference between the potential service providers, so she chose Thunderbolt IT because she felt she could trust and work with Jonathan Forstein, the VP of sales. Jeremy was uncertain about how Thunderbolt IT's processes justified a higher price, so he went with the cheapest option.

All three talked about the huge amount of information they consumed on the web—and how people were emailing them asking for an appointment. They each attended a webinar around IT services and asked for advice from friends or colleagues in similar situations. While they had a ton of information, to a person, they felt as if no one really took the time to get to know them, their business, or their specific IT challenges.

The way they described how they felt during their buyer journey definitely sounded like they were in a swirling cyclone.

The one bright spot of Julie's week was that Bonnie McAllister started as the new CMO on Monday. *Maybe she has some insight into this situation?*

Bonnie was there before Julie on Monday morning—a good sign.

After giving Bonnie a pleasant welcome coffee and a tour around Thunderbolt IT's offices, she asked her to meet in the conference room at 11:00 a.m.

"Bonnie, I have a feeling that your first day will be a milestone for our company," Julie began.

Bonnie smiled. "Me too."

She summarized her mentorship conversations of the past few weeks, then asked Bonnie what she thought about those discussions and Sam's advice.

"He sure sounds like he knows what he's talking about," Bonnie began. "Based on my experience with marketing professional services like IT, there is definitely a large volume of noise surrounding the purchase. I have been successful mapping out the prospect journey and making sure our marketing and sales touches and tactics create a remarkable and educational experience. This helps position us as the thought leader, guide, and trusted advisor. I also like his description of the 'Cyclonic Buyer Journey.' It is certainly an accurate way to describe how the environment impacts the way people buy today. I am also very familiar with the tactics necessary to engage with prospects earlier in their buyer journey. Let me put some suggestions together and have something tomorrow for you to consider."

Julie smiled without even realizing it.

The next morning, they met again in the conference room.

"How was the rest of your first day, Bonnie?" asked Julie.

"It was a cyclone!" Bonnie joked. "All kidding aside, it was excellent. I talked with several team members, to orient myself, and have come to a conclusion: Thunderbolt IT has a fabulous inside reality, but we stink at telling our story. I'm going to fix the bridge between all of the amazing things we do for clients and what the outside perception of our firm is, ASAP. I'll need you to do a little strategy work over the next few weeks to help us really tell our story—as well as differentiate us from the competition. I always like to create the recipe before I bake the cake!

"But you asked me to help with some marketing campaign ideas that consider the buyer journey, so I thought we should start at the beginning. Let's target people who don't know we exist but who probably have challenges that we can fix—people who are unaware that solutions are available, people in the Pre-awareness stage. I pulled out an account-based marketing plan that I used for my last company. We had success introducing ourselves to prospects who (1) didn't know about us and (2) didn't even know they had problems. With your approval, I'll tailor it to our company. Basically, there are eight components."

Bonnie walked Julie through the plan.

Start with the Data

"If we have bad data, we'll have ineffective marketing campaigns, so we have to make sure our data is complete, accurate, and clean. We have to look at our CRM and marketing automation databases to make sure our contact data is accurate. We might need to supplement our databases with additional data to make the marketing more personal and effective. We also have to make sure our CRM and marketing automation products are mapped and integrated correctly. Prospect and customer data should flow back and forth seamlessly, with no duplication and no extra effort on the part of our people."

Targeting Whales

"The goal of marketing tactics like this is to spearfish for whales. We're going to want to identify the five hundred biggest target accounts we want to go after proactively, then the individual people we want to talk with at those companies. This is why the data has to be so clean—because if we start outreach and the data is bad, we'll look unorganized and foolish.

"I took a look in our CRM and identified two hundred companies that fit the profile for a whale. We'll find a data source to supplement that with another three hundred companies, including contact information. We need more than one contact at each company—probably more like four or five. We'll want the CEOs, the influencers, the traditional champion titles (like CIO or CTO), and the financial leaders (CFOs). We might want operational contacts, too, if we're going to tell an efficiency-gains story; those ops people will like that."

Wow, Julie thought. Bonnie knew what she was doing, and her approach was well-thought-out and systematic. *This is already going in the right direction.* "Keep going," Julie said. "I like what I hear so far."

Creating the Content to Connect with Targeted People at Targeted Accounts

"Two of the major keys to account-based marketing (ABM), when creating content to disrupt the status quo of people whose attention we want to gain, are relevance and personalization. We need to create campaigns and offers that are personalized to our particular targets. Plus, we need to develop specific content for each of our target personas: the CEOs, CIOs, CFOs, and the operational contacts. Each of them will have different perspectives—and maybe even different goals when working with a company like ours. For example, a lot of our value comes from slashing expenses for our clients; this resonates with the CFO. We also drive efficiency for our clients, which appeals to the COO. For the CEO, we can talk about how we empower teams to innovate more dramatically—you know, big picture stuff.

"It's going to take some time, but we need to go persona by persona and create disruptive, emotional, and compelling messages that will shake them out of their status quo. Then we need content that we can offer to get them to connect with us. Remember, they don't know us. Finally, we need content that gets them excited enough to engage in a conversation—via marketing initially, but we'll want to work to get them interested in talking directly to sales soon afterward. We'll control their buyer journey, cutting out competition and quickly gaining their trust. They'll want to do business with us instead of us trying to sell them on the idea.

"How does that sound Julie?"

"Are you kidding? It sounds great. We've never done anything like this—but how long are we talking about before this starts producing results?"

Sales and Marketing Alignment

Bonnie continued: "Now, understand that most marketers are driven by a desire to create sales-ready leads, and they ignore the equally qualified prospects who are early in their buyer journey. So, we're attempting to go after people who are not even looking for a new IT service provider. You're going to have to be patient as we educate, guide, and advise these people.

"We're also going to want to align sales and marketing completely. No partial alignment. For account-based marketing campaigns to work, you need one hundred percent alignment. Jonathan and I are going to have to be one mind. Targeting and selection, execution scripts and playbooks, content delivery, sales process, tracking metrics, ongoing training, closed loop feedback from sales to marketing, and even the technology we use to automate execution. All of it. Are you supportive of that, Julie?"

Julie responded quickly: "One hundred percent— whatever you need. Just let me know how I can help."

Content for the Entire Buyer Journey— but Especially for the Back End of a Prospect's Journey

Bonnie continued: "The early-buyer-journey content is great, but if I want to keep Jonathan happy, we're going to need to produce more sales-ready leads, more people who want to talk to our sales team. To do that, we'll need much better late-stage-buyer-journey offers. 'Contact us,' 'speak with a rep,' and 'schedule a free consultation' are not cutting it: we need to upgrade these offers. The good news is that this work can usually be planned and implemented pretty quickly.

"Let me give you a couple of examples. Instead of 'schedule a consultation,' let's upgrade that offer to 'a free thirty-minute IT assessment.' In thirty minutes, we'll give prospects three or four ideas they can execute today to improve their IT infrastructure, their security, or their support. If we come up with a couple more of those, and then make sure sales can execute those conversations, we should be able to produce more sales-ready leads in no time. Having the right offers for early-, mid-, and late-stage-buyer-journey prospects will be key to getting results from our ABM campaign, too."

Using Social Media

"Since we're going after people we don't know, we'll need social media to get their contact information. In some cases, we'll start the outreach via social networks— LinkedIn, specifically.

"We can use LinkedIn and Twitter to do outreach and try to connect, but we can also pay for ads to appear when they log on to LinkedIn. This narrow campaign will support our other demand generation efforts without spending too much on advertising. It will also give us some air support when our sales reps reach out individually. They should have already heard of Thunderbolt, if we do this correctly."

By this point, Julie was beyond glad she'd had the foresight to bring Bonnie on board.

Start a 3-D Mail Campaign

The new CMO continued: "As digital marketing rose in popularity, direct mail was left for dead. But today, we can use direct to reach our targeted executives. The high-level executives we need to get in front of don't register for webinars, download white papers, respond to unsolicited emails, or follow companies on Twitter as much as we would prefer, so we can use direct mail to attack them from a different angle.

"At my old job, we used a '10-10-10' tactic: 10 introductory calls, 10 '3-D mail' packages, and then 10 follow-up calls per salesperson per week. If we take our list of 200 targeted companies and multiply by 5 contacts in each company, that's 1,000 contacts we have to touch. If we divide them by Thunderbolt's six salespeople and attack ten of them each week, we can introduce ourselves to all of our prospects within the next four to five months.

"We ship ten packages per salesperson per week on Monday. We send them via guaranteed two-day shipping. That way, we know they arrive no later than Wednesday. Each package will contain content to tweak the prospect's pain. Just thinking off the cuff, we could do something like sending a box of peanuts with a handwritten note that says, 'If worrying about your network's security is driving you *nuts*, we should talk.' It sounds silly, but you'd be amazed how effective it is.

"The same day, we want each salesperson to call the ten prospects on their respective list after-hours. We're hoping for voice mail so that we can leave a message that says, 'Hi, this is Tom calling from Thunderbolt IT. I just wanted to let you know that I sent you a package and I'll follow up on Thursday morning.' We want our prospects to hear the name of the company and be aware that something was sent to them.

"Now on Thursday morning, the sales team follows up with this introduction: 'Hi, I'm Tom, the guy that sent you a box of peanuts. I would love to schedule a time to talk with you about your cybersecurity, IT infrastructure, or hardware support and see if we can help you solve your most pressing IT challenges.' If the prospect does not want to talk—sales, right—then we can drop back; maybe we offer to register them for an upcoming webinar or send them a white paper. At the end of the day, activity breeds activity."

"Wow, Bonnie," Julie remarked. "You've really got this planned out, don't you?"

"Marketing is about one plus one equaling three. We want to get as many campaign tactics firing simultaneously as possible and then orchestrate them all to create the experience we've been talking about. It's complicated, but when you get it set up, it works like a charm."

End with the Data

"For the last part of the ABM program and our Pre-awareness campaign, the focus is on metrics and technology. We need to create dashboards with key metrics to gain insight into whether the execution is working as expected. No matter how many times I've done this, it's always a little unique, and we'll need ongoing optimization based on data to really get it to hum.

"We'll want to look at total contacts, connect rates, engagement rates, and conversions from contact to sales opportunity—and then track the sales ops through the sales process to see who is closing. We'll also want to see how our ABM content is performing and make adjustments along the way. What gets measured gets done. We have to track everything.

"I also talked about technology. We'll use marketing automation and CRM tools to run this, but we might need some ABM technology, too. I'm going to wait and see how we're doing before recommending any investment here, but solutions like Engagio and Terminus can help us execute our playbook and serve up ads to targeted execs. Hold that thought for now."

Bonnie wrapped up with, "If we execute this plan, it will be virtually impossible for us *not* to generate business from this targeted list. It might take thirty to ninety days, but we'll be proactively reaching out to our perfectly profiled prospects the entire time."

Julie said, "Bonnie, this all sounds great. What do you need from me to get started?"

"I've spoken to Amber Lee about her work as a marketing campaign manager. I'd like to bring her in to help with the work. She is more than capable of executing many of these tactics, if I help her with the strategy. We're already on the HubSpot platform, but we've only really used the software for email marketing. I'll show Amber Lee all of the modules, and she can begin to really utilize the tool to help make the work easier and more effective—plus start to give us insights into the data."

Julie's smile said it all: the healing had begun!

4

A PROBLEM FOR ANOTHER DAY: THE CYCLONE OF AWARENESS

A mailman was going door to door, delivering his letters. When he came to Farmer Brown's house, he found the old man in a rocking chair on his front porch, reading the paper, a hound dog lying at his feet.

Farmer Brown and the mailman chatted for a bit. While they did, the mailman noticed the dog whining and whimpering the whole time.

Finally, he asked the old man, "What's wrong with your dog?"

Farmer Brown replied, "Oh, he's lying on a nail."

"Well, why don't he move?"

The old man frowned thoughtfully and said,
"I reckon it don't hurt enough."

—UNKNOWN

NASA says our sun has only about 4.5 billion more years of life.

Is it something we should really worry about? Maybe . . . but we don't. The idea of the star that anchors our solar system going supernova and eventually dying is a problem, but it's not an imminent one. If you're a normal person, you're probably more concerned about what you're going to do for dinner tonight.

On the one hand, we're talking about the fate of the human race. On the other hand, 4.5 billion years is a long, long time from now, whereas dinner is in a matter of hours. When we weigh it in the balance, dinner is more important than trying to figure out a solution to a dying sun.

Then, of course, there's the question of effectiveness. Aside from some NASA scientists or maybe the late Stephen Hawking, few of us are equipped to even begin addressing that problem, much less solve it.

There's also the issue of urgency. Why do we need to solve this problem here in the twenty-first century? Future generations will be better equipped with the information and technology to handle this problem. After all, humanity has at least a few million years or so to figure it out.

This just isn't something normal people worry about.

So let's bring the discussion a little closer to home and discuss a challenge that will happen in our lifetime, not just to collective humanity but to each of us as individuals—living out our golden years.

Unless you plan to die with a hammer in your hand,

you don't want to work your entire life. We all hope to retire from actively participating in the workforce, and each of us needs a plan for how we're going to support ourselves (and maybe even our loved ones) during those years to come.

Why, then, does the Economic Policy Institute find that nearly half—*half!*—of American adults have zero dollars in savings?[17] Zip. Zilch. Nada. For those few who actually have planned and saved for retirement, the median family has saved just $60,000. (Yes, that includes individual retirement accounts, 401(k)s, and other investment vehicles.) The median savings for people between fifty-six and sixty-one years old (i.e., those nearing traditional retirement years) is just $17,000. You can't even buy a new Buick for seventeen grand, much less live out retirement.

But if you were to take a survey, you would hear, yes, everyone plans to retire. Yes, they know they need to save up for retirement. Yes, they know they don't have enough. Yes, that's a problem.

But like the sun going supernova, it's a problem for another day.

Nero Fiddled While Rome Burned: The Complacency of Awareness

If we were to create an avatar of someone in the Awareness cyclone, it would be a fifty-six-year-old man who

17   Monique Morrissey, "The State of American Retirement: How 401(k)s Have Failed Most American Workers," Economic Policy Institute, March 3, 2016, https://www.epi.org/publication/retirement-in-america/#charts.

would, in just under a decade, ride off into the sunset with all of $17,000 in his wallet.

Knowing that retirement is coming up in just a few short years, why doesn't he squirrel away more? Why not cut back his personal budget to the bone? Why not pick up a second job? Why not find a better financial planner?

We're not talking about people who've faced unique hardships or financial misfortune. Some situations are beyond control. Here, we're talking about your every-day, suburban-living, Sunday-football-watching, pick-up-driving, down-to-earth, average Joe. Why is he grilling steaks and drinking a beer when he has less than a decade before he plans to retire *with $17,000*!?

When you think of someone in the Awareness cyclone, that's who you should picture: someone aware that they have a problem, but "gee, you know, I should probably do something about that sometime."

It's worse when we move into the business realm, where executives may be at greater fault than Average Joe here. Joe might be forgiven for keeping his head down and trudging through the daily grind, not appreciating how quickly time is slipping by. Business leaders, on the other hand, are paid precisely to see ahead and plan for the future. Yet in industry after industry, we watch as leaders not only fail to see opportunities for innovation but fail to react to disruption even after the new course of an indus-try has been inevitably set.

In 1993 the *New York Times* bought the *Boston Globe*

for a breathtaking $1.1 billion, only to sell it twenty years later for a jaw-dropping $70 million. You can forgive the *Times* for failing to grasp in 1993 just how world changing the emerging mystery of "the Internet thing" was going to be. But after a few years, and especially after daily papers began falling like flies only to be bought and merged into ever larger consolidated media groups, the *Times* should have seen the writing on the wall. The paper needed to change strategies, desperately. It didn't.

It's been the same story in music, publishing, and scores of other industries. Despite the warning bells, despite the winds of change, despite watching their competitors being snatched up by global conglomerates, most business leaders just hunker down and hope to ride out the storm in one piece.

This is a gross oversimplification, of course. It's far more difficult to fundamentally change the culture and workings of a staid institution like the *Boston Globe* than it is for Average Joe to get serious about retirement planning. But at both the consumer level and the business level, you find people aware of a problem but doing next to nothing about it.

Why Do People Wait to Take Action?

Why do people put off doing something about a problem they know they have? This question delves far deeper into psychology than any of us probably want to go. But on a pragmatic level, we find that these are the main reasons that we need be concerned with in business.

Feeling overwhelmed: Starting out, plenty of self-employed professionals are dimly aware that they should have an accounting system. But setting a system up, finding a bookkeeper or accountant, figuring out taxes—it just seems like so much to tackle that they push it out of their mind until it's tax time, and then they *have* to do something about it. It's easier to ignore something than to sit down for even a few minutes to learn how to solve it.

Lack of immediacy: This may be the culprit behind so many industries imploding. Intellectually, business leaders and managers may know that they need to change course to avoid the fate of their peers, but emotionally, they're complacent. Bad things may be coming, but it doesn't *feel* like there's impending doom; it just feels like another Tuesday.

Fear of responsibility: Especially in the workplace, many people fear putting time toward a problem because they're afraid they'll get saddled with the full responsibility of it, even if they just wanted to help get the ball rolling . . . which also means they'll get saddled with the blame if it falls through. It's easier to not rock the boat.

Not invented here or not my problem: Just because someone recognizes a problem doesn't mean that they recognize it as a problem for themselves. A restaurateur may not care that a street renovation project will cause the other members of the downtown merchants association to lose foot traffic and business, until he looks at the map and realizes that the project will extend to his block as well. Suddenly he feels charitable and decides to donate to the association's lobbying efforts.

Underestimation and misconception: Sometimes people stay in the cyclone of Awareness because they believe that whatever problem they have is smaller or easier than it really is. Many business owners are shocked to learn that an effective web marketing campaign, for instance, can easily take six months to assemble. In the car-buying example from chapter two, the buyer had no idea that college tuition had risen so dramatically. (In 1997 annual tuition at a public out-of-state university averaged $8,840; by 2017 it had tripled to $26,010.[18] Quite the cause for shell shock.)

Comparatively low priority: Something gets pushed to the proverbial back burner because there are too many other needs that take precedence. When a company forecasts lower earnings for next year, the execs at the top may decide their fleet isn't quite as old as they thought; they put off replacing it in favor of setting profits aside against future losses.

Fear of change: This is the most common reason people never move out of the Awareness stage. Sometimes doing nothing feels safer than doing something. Humans

18   Briana Boyington, "See 20 Years of Tuition Growth at National Universities," *U.S. News and World Report*, September 20, 2017, https://www.usnews.com/education/best-colleges/paying-for-college/articles/2017-09-20/see-20-years-of-tuition-growth-at-national-universities.

are genetically designed to fear change and stay away from it. Not a single month goes by where we don't meet a CEO who knows their business is not growing, knows their marketing is not working, knows their sales effort is ineffective, yet investing in a better way is something they don't seem to be able to do. The fear of that risk is seemingly beyond their physical, mental, and emotional capabilities.

Faced with this inertia, how do you influence your buyer to take action?

The Fear of Loss

"Hear what you've been missing."

Those five little words made all the difference in Bose's sales of its Wave music system. Before that, the company's marketing had focused on its revolutionary innovation, its patented technology, and the wonderful listening experience people reported. The system, however, cost much more than what people were used to paying. Trying to convince them how much better a Wave system was didn't work. But adding those five words activated one of our most primal fears: the fear of missing out, known by its slang acronym "FOMO" (not to be confused with "mofo").

While Bose should certainly advertise its innovative tech, using it as a differentiator in the marketplace, that alone failed to spur action. Once Bose framed its tech as the answer to something you didn't even know you were missing, though, the company became the undisputed leader in luxury audio technology. In fact, this could even be used as an example of reaching potential buyers in the Pre-awareness cyclone because Bose's future customers didn't even know there was a problem. It was only by the company pointing out that they had been missing something that it spurred them to investigate further.

Disrupt their thinking. Trigger their fear. Hit the FOMO.

THUNDERBOLT IT

Sam said, "Good morning, Julie. You seem chipper today!"

"You think so? I guess I must be feeling a bit better than the first time we met for coffee."

"Oh? Why is that?"

Julie proceeded to update Sam on all of the things Bonnie had suggested for Thunderbolt IT over the last week.

"Looks like Bonnie is a keeper," Sam observed. "She seems to have insight into the psychology of sales and marketing. That will help us cure your company's growth challenges. Plus, the tactics she's putting into place to help your prospects in the Pre-awareness cyclone are right on point. Very exciting!"

Julie agreed, "Yes, I look forward to my huddles with her—and I only just met her. The first week couldn't have gone any better, in my opinion. Next week, she has put some time on the calendar to work on our messaging. She wants to dive deeper into the personas of our clients and prospects—to really start developing some ways we can differentiate ourselves through the stories we tell with our marketing and sales conversations."

"Strategy is the secret sauce, hands down," Sam confirmed. "Her looking to strategy before executing tactics is the right approach. Let's talk about the next cyclone we have to help people navigate through: it's called Awareness. Before, we discussed that Pre-awareness is when prospects don't know about your company or the solutions you offer—solutions that could help eliminate their problems. This cyclone is slightly different. In Awareness, people know they have a problem, but they're still *not* actively looking for a solution. However, they are open to information; they are aware there's an issue; their reticular activation system is on."

"What the heck is that?" Julie asked.

"Okay, remember when you bought your last car and then started noticing how many people were driving the same car? That's the reticular activation system working. Your prospects have the same situation. Once they're aware of a situation, issue, or challenge, they're noticing stuff they ignored before. They might even take a few actions, like running a quick search or two. They're not yet ready to invest time and money to find a solution, but they are aware solutions exist, and they are more open to marketing messages and content offers."

"I get it. That makes a lot of sense, and I love how we're using the human brain and the psychology of purchasing to design our marketing." Julie was very excited.

"Even though prospects in this stage of the buyer journey are aware solutions exist—and that they might have a problem worth looking at—the noise and confusion is still very high. You and Bonnie have to create the interactions that help buyers focus, filter out the noise, and hear your story."

Sam continued: "No purchase is ever made unless it makes pain less acute. Think about your own purchasing behavior. Do you ever buy something if you don't need it or want it? Of course not.

"At this stage, your prospects might not have acute pain yet. So your content, advice, and guidance have to be designed to poke at pain and help them understand the potential challenges facing them down the road if they don't take action.

"Julie, your homework this week is to discuss this with Bonnie and then let me know how she plans to capture people in the Awareness stage. Also, I'm curious to see what you guys develop with regard to differentiation and compelling messaging."

"Sam, thank you so much for all of your help and encouragement. I really appreciate you taking the time."

"I'm enjoying seeing someone else's success. See you next week!" he replied.

Deep in thought, Julie took the long way back to the office. While it seemed like a lot of work, she was starting to see the *method* to the madness of sales and marketing. She was kicking herself that she hadn't explored these topics more deeply before. She realized that she would have a far larger business if she had made these changes a few years ago.

"Water under the bridge." She sighed as she turned into Thunderbolt's parking lot.

Julie recapped her morning meeting with Bonnie and asked her to develop a set of recommendations for this new stage, just as she had done with Pre-awareness. A few days later, they met to discuss her ideas.

Bonnie opened with an encouraging statement: "Inbound marketing will help us move folks through the Awareness cyclone. Luckily, inbound is my specialty."

Bonnie explained that she agreed with Sam about the way people buy today and had solutions for how to capture them and turn them into sales opportunities. The first step was to create content to offer on their website—and to look at the site to make sure the entire content experience was remarkable and easy to navigate. She suggested starting with a collection of educational offers: one white paper, one infographic, and one video, each focusing on a different pain point that a prospective client might have. She could get Amber Lee to work on creating the landing pages for each offer.

Then Bonnie requested they strategically place the offers on the pages that were designed to connect with prospects in the Awareness stage. "To make it as frictionless as possible, I think we should simply ask for their email address—no complicated forms or company information to enter. Because the prospects are early in their buyer journey, they're not ready to give up all their contact information. They don't want to talk to anyone yet, so we have to only ask for their email address. This will ensure the highest possible conversion rate—and that we'll collect a lot of email addresses. We can then nurture those over time, and we'll talk about that nurture plan later on.

"We'll use HubSpot (our marketing automation and CRM software) to collect the email addresses, and then we'll set up some automated email nurture campaigns to stay in touch with these people over the next week or so. Julie, are you okay if we test different messages and lengths to see which produce the best set of results?"

"Of course. You seem to have an excellent handle on all aspects of the campaigns you've described to me. The testing seems like a great idea—can't wait to see what comes out of it."

Bonnie explained that there would be three to six touchpoints for each nurture campaign, and each campaign would be offer specific. She based the timing on the historical sales cycle length—in Thunderbolt IT's case, about six months. She also explained that, in each of the nurture emails, there would be additional offers designed to help signal to the Thunderbolt IT marketing and sales team if a prospect was moving through the buyer journey.

Bonnie also broached the subject of getting found on

the Internet via search. She explained to Julie that no work had been done to their current website to make sure it was designed to rank on Google (and other search engines) for specific search terms and keywords—the keywords prospects who buy IT services were using. She suggested a parallel effort: upgrade the current website so that it would rank more frequently (and for the right keywords), and initiate a search engine marketing (SEM) campaign. She wanted to use LinkedIn Sponsored Updates and Google AdWords to drive leads while the search engine optimization work got done in the background. Organically ranking on Google took time, while the paid social ads and the Google AdWords campaign had the potential to impact results immediately.

"Eventually, I'd like to wean us off of paid search completely, once the organic results are at an acceptable level," she noted.

Basing her goal on their historical site-wide conversion rate of a half percent, Bonnie set a target of one percent conversion. Given an average landing page conversion rate of twenty percent, she wanted to get that to forty percent. "If these goals are attained, we'll double our lead generation from the website. And when all of this is complete, we will have taken the first steps to converting website visitors into leads during the Awareness phase of the buyers' journey," Bonnie declared.

This was far exceeding Julie's expectations, and she was thrilled. She shared her enthusiasm with Bonnie, who reiterated, "Everything we do is going to be measured and optimized, and I'll walk you through the reports myself. You'll be well versed in reading website conversion data in no time!"

5

"WHERE DO I EVEN START?": THE CYCLONE OF EDUCATION

The reason most people don't get what they want
is because they don't know what they want.

—T. HARV EKER

Remember Enron?

That financial scandal rocked Wall Street so hard that it became a textbook example of how even in a relatively well-regulated financial system like the United States, you could get by with billions upon billions of dollars in fraud. In less than a year, Congress passed the Sarbanes-Oxley

Act, a wide-sweeping regulatory bill, to protect investors from future Enron-type corruption, as well as pierce the corporate veil to hold executive managers and board members personally responsible for the acts of public companies. Sarbanes-Oxley also gave the Securities and Exchange Commission (SEC) authority to further create and define those regulations going forward.

The potential of jail time . . . "motivated," shall we say, executives to make sure their company fully complied with the new regulations. Because of how quickly the new law was passed, coupled with new directives continually being issued by the SEC, it caught corporations and accountants off guard. (For frame of reference of just how quickly Sarbanes-Oxley was passed, Congress passed the Homeland Security Act in November 2002 in response to September 11 just thirteen months before; it passed Sarbanes-Oxley in July 2002 in response to Enron's bankruptcy just eight months before.)

There was a mad scramble to learn the law and to bring corporate accounting up to code, creating huge market opportunities for companies like Enterprise Financial Consulting (EFC), a ten-office, nationwide accounting consultancy. Unfortunately, "huge market opportunities" equals huge competition. EFC's message got lost in the sea of hundreds of competing accounting firms, not to mention the then industry giants of Ernst & Young, Deloitte, Arthur Andersen, KPMG, and PricewaterhouseCoopers.

When EFC first started working with us, its marketing

was of the traditional variety: mass advertising in expensive trade magazines targeting C-suite execs of public companies (and especially chief financial officers), with their messaging focused on the company's years of experience, their expertise, and their national presence.

Put yourself in the shoes of a CFO at a $100 million public company (the typical size at an initial public offering). You are more than aware of your pain; you are downright terrified. If you can't get the company compliant with Sarbanes-Oxley by the SEC-mandated deadlines, you could face personal repercussions. The situation has your full and undivided attention. You are more than motivated to do something about this problem. You are desperately trying to get a handle on the situation.

But what should you do?

It seems like every other article in *CFO* magazine talks about Sarbanes-Oxley, and some of them even contradict each other! You have a hundred pieces of mail from accounting firms you've never heard of offering you their services. The sales reps from KPMG, Ernst & Young, and Arthur Andersen are begging for follow-up appointments. You have a dozen emails from your in-house accountants who want to go to different seminars or conferences that feature Sarbanes-Oxley compliance information. The CEO and board of directors want a full compliance strategy update by quarter's end. The ideas and possibilities whirl around in your head, inducing anxiety like you haven't had since grad school.

As you read the latest issue of *CFO*, you see one full-color spread after another of firms touting their expertise with Sarbanes-Oxley. You recognize some of the names from the pile of mail on your desk, but most you've never heard of. What are you doing to do?

The old adage comes to mind: "Nobody ever got fired for hiring IBM." With something like this, maybe it'd be best to hire one of the big accounting firms . . . just to CYA. They're incredibly expensive, but you can't go wrong with them. They have their reputations for a reason, right?

Now, step out of the CFO's shoes. Enterprise Financial Consulting's expensive magazine ad didn't grab their attention. It spoke to their pain—"specializing in Sarbanes-Oxley corporate compliance"—but it did nothing to influence them in the midst of their Education cyclone.

No wonder the company's phones weren't ringing.

The True Aim of Education

HubSpot CEO Brian Halligan once said, "Your success with inbound marketing and sales is much more dependent on the size of your brain than the size of your wallet." In other words, work smarter, not harder.

As we said earlier, when professional marketers talk about the education phase of the sales funnel, they're generally talking about what they do to the prospect: educate the buyer on the products and services they offer. If they possess even a little marketing savvy, they position their content one step removed. In this instance, they might suggest that EFC "educate" prospects by providing information on "how to choose the right accounting firm for you" or something else that's basically a thinly disguised ad for its own firm.

The true aim of education is not to give the buyer information on your products and services, even if it's under the guise of "educational material" or "content." That's often a gimmick and one that you've no doubt seen: a blog post that compares different vendors but written in such a way that leaves only one logical choice, or a magazine article that looks like an editorial but has the words "SPONSORED CONTENT" printed in tiny font at the top of the page. That's simply repackaged advertising.

Your efforts to influence the buyer in the Education cyclone should focus around two drivers: help them better understand their problem and provide them the information they're looking for (instead of only the content you want to give them) on the ways they can address that pain.

With EFC, we dug deeper into CFOs' pain and discovered that one of their main challenges was trying to get audit controls in place by the SEC's deadline. We advised the company's leadership that this was the pain point they should address, that they should build an entire marketing campaign around it, and that they should immediately drop the expensive magazine ads.

We were prepared to hear their version of what we almost always hear:

- "We don't want to sell audit control planning. That's just one small part of the services we provide!"
- "If we teach them how to do it themselves, what do they need us for?"
- "We have to have our ads—if we don't, people will think we've gone out of business!"

Fortunately, their leadership was quite open to doing something new. After all, what they had been doing wasn't working. Together, we created a free webinar titled "6 Ways to Create an Effective Sarbanes-Oxley Compliance Program in 29 Days." For a fraction of a magazine ad's cost, we created the webinar program, marketed it for them, and drove registrations. EFC's team provided intelligent educational content in the emails leading up to the webinar and then personally presented the content, implicitly positioning the firm as the experts for such.

Was it successful? Are you kidding? In the midst of the cyclone swirling with the litany of worries and problems that the CFOs were facing, here was an expert offering complimentary information on how to deal with one of their most pressing problems. CFOs couldn't sign up fast enough!

Did every one of them become a client? No. In fact, only a fraction of the total attendees reached out for additional information, much less became paying customers.

Did most of them use the information EFC provided in lieu of hiring them or someone else to do audit controls? Yes. It wouldn't have been an honest educational tool if the webinar didn't actually do what its title implied. Did the webinar have ROI? Absolutely. In fact, because EFC dropped the print ads, it could easily track the source of new leads and then calculate a simple ROI to demonstrate exactly how much of its revenue came from those webinars, including the two six-figure clients who signed up after the very first one.

Years later the firm was sold to an even larger firm (the fourth of our clients to achieve their goal of being acquired). While we can't take the credit for that, having a resoundingly successful marketing machine able to measure its direct top-line revenue certainly didn't hurt.

The reason it was a resounding success wasn't because the webinars were a good idea—it was due to the company's leadership fully embracing the spirit of helping their prospects in their Education cyclone. In the webinars, they didn't try to "sell, sell, sell!" They didn't break the attendees' trust by turning the webinar into an infomercial. They didn't try to slyly slip in references to the company's success and its long history. They didn't use the webinar as a tease to get them to sign up for a paid webinar or a "complimentary consultation" (read: meeting with a salesperson) for the rest of the content.

They focused on educating attendees. What a novel idea.

The Science and Spirit of Reciprocity

At first blush, EFC's free webinars accomplish quite a bit. They provide a low- to no-risk offer, an excuse to stay in touch with prospects, a means to speak directly to CFOs on a personal level, and a way to clearly yet implicitly establish the firm's credibility and expertise. These days, giving away free content and providing similar webinars like this is Sales & Marketing 101.

But there's a deeper reason behind why genuinely educational material with no strings attached works so well, regardless of whether your prospect is B2B or B2C: reciprocity.

In two of his profoundly insightful books, *Influence: The Psychology of Persuasion* and the later *Pre-Suasion: A Revolutionary Way to Influence and Persuade,* psychologist Robert Cialdini addresses how humans are biologically hardwired to respond to generosity. (Adam Grant's *Give and Take: Why Helping Others Drives Our Success* also provides concrete and compelling writing on the subject.)

When someone gives us a gift or does us a favor, we automatically feel more warmly toward them and compelled to reciprocate. It's genetic. Cialdini talks about the possibly evolutionary reasons for these feelings, but regardless of why, they're instinctual and universal. When given something gratuitously, we feel an obligation to somehow return the favor.

Charities have known and practiced this for years. The reason they send you free personalized address labels isn't because they want to save you the hassle of writing your return address on your mail; it's because they have greater fundraising success when they give a free gift and tap into that subconscious need to return the favor.

The Hare Krishnas knew this long before Cialdini published *Influence* in 1984. Are you old enough to remember them thronging you in the airport, pressing you to take a flower? Even if you wouldn't accept, some of them would go so far as to stick one in your lapel or pocket. Why? Because even if the Hare Krishnas annoyed some people, they still got more donations by giving something as simple as a flower.

Even being aware himself of how reciprocity worked didn't make Cialdini immune to its effects. In *Pre-Suasion*, he wrote about how he had intended to finish the book several years earlier. He had taken a leave of absence from his multiple responsibilities at his university and opted for a light teaching role at a distant business school for a semester. With the easier schedule, he looked forward to months of productive writing. In preparing to relocate, he was negotiating with an associate dean in a series of emails regarding the final details of his visit. One day, instead of a reply, Cialdini received a phone call.

> "Bob," [the associate dean] said, "I have good news. I was able to get you the office you wanted; the computer in there is more powerful than the one you asked for; don't worry about access to a secretary, the

library, parking, long-distance calls—we'll take care of all that." I was grateful and told him how much I appreciated all he'd done for me. He waited a beat and replied, "Well, there's something you could do for me. We've just experienced the need for someone to teach a specialized marketing class for our MBA students. I'm in a bind, and it would really help me out if you could do it."

I knew that agreeing to his request would torpedo my chances of completing the planned book during my stay . . . [but] I agreed anyway. I couldn't see any other appropriate option, not in the instant after expressing my sincere thanks for everything [he] had just provided.[19]

This beautiful meta-example shows how even being an expert on the subject of reciprocity (while even writing another book about it!) didn't stop his own feelings of obligation from instantly making him say yes to a request that would negate his whole reason for taking the leave of absence in the first place.

This automatic reciprocity doesn't kick in if the person on the receiving end feels that you're trying to sell something. It's why obvious advertisements don't have the same effect as content aimed at providing genuine

---

19 Robert Cialdini, *Pre-Suasion: A Revolutionary Way to Influence and Persuade* (New York: Simon & Schuster, 2016).

information to your prospects. This feeling is one of the main reasons EFC's free webinars were so effective. The company was providing something of value to CFOs with no strings attached, invoking subconscious feelings of likability and obligation.

We even have these feelings toward disembodied brands. One of our clients told us about their experience with MeetEdgar, a service that schedules social media posts. He posted a minor recommendation to their help desk. In a matter of minutes, one of their customer service reps not only thanked him for that recommendation specifically (versus a generic "Thank you for your feedback!" message) but also gave him a link to go "Snag yourself some Edgar SWAG for taking the time to give us a feature update!" The linked page gave him the option of getting a T-shirt, tote bag, or beanie and having it shipped to his office for free.

"I loved them before anyway, but this just made me feel it that much more," he said.

He wouldn't have experienced those same feelings toward the company if they had offered a trade upfront: "Tell us what you think and you can get something for free." When something is a trade, it's not free. He would have felt that he'd earned the T-shirt (or tote or whatever he picked).

Likewise, if EFC had offered access to the webinar as a trade, perhaps in exchange for a fifteen-minute phone call with a sales rep, the CFOs who did attend wouldn't feel that they somehow owed the company; they would be trading something. The webinars were far more effective precisely because EFC offered them for nothing.

Educate, then let your buyer feel the need to reciprocate.

What to Educate Them About

You have primarily two ways to approach the content of your education efforts. You can provide information to help your potential buyers better understand their problem, and you can provide information around potential solutions to that problem.

For instance, in making our own proprietary software, we found ourselves in the Education cyclone on how to go about a software project. Because we're business revenue generation guys, we'd never gotten into software development, so we imagined that we would probably hire a company to do the programming on our behalf, as we had intended when we first thought about doing something like this ten years ago.

But software development is quite a different animal these days than it used to be. A decade ago, if you wanted to create custom software, you outsourced the whole thing to one company. Today, all it takes is a simple Google search—"how do I create my own software"—and *boom!* Options, ideas, advice, resources, articles, and more. In our case, while in the Education cyclone, we weren't ready to hire a company. We needed information on what we should be doing in the first place. We gravitated to books, magazine articles, and blog posts that talked about how it's done today, what we should know before we got into it, "if I could do it over again" pieces that would help us avoid common pitfalls and mistakes, and all the different routes we could take.

Plenty of the content we read had been written by helpful IT professionals with nothing to sell. They simply wanted to help other people out there figure out how to do it right. These kinds of freely giving people are what make the world go round. (See how high an opinion we have of complete strangers who provide something for free? That's reciprocity!) There were also companies who were great sources of information, and the ones we trusted the most were those whose advice was backed up by others and who provided genuine advice without trying to push their own products and services.

Some of this information addressed the first high-level topic by helping us better understand our problem and how to avoid loss. The rest of the information we found addressed the other high-level topic by helping us understand our options and the respective advantages of each.

EFC's webinars focused on one aspect of its buyers' pain with their audit controls. Because of the ultracompetitive market it found itself in, providing free content about how to become Sarbanes-Oxley compliant was too broad. It wouldn't have been enough to cut through all the noise of the free seminars and complimentary consultations its competitors offered. By focusing on one particular aspect of the buyers' pain (i.e., by going deep instead of broad) CFOs were signing up by the dozens.

Here's the rub: all those freely giving people actually add to the noise of the buyer's cyclone. According to Nielsen and other sources, the amount of content we consume on a daily basis has grown from two hours a day in the 1920s to nearly eleven hours today. The cyclone isn't calming down. Quite the opposite: it's growing more violent. If you want to cut through the clutter and influence your buyer more effectively, you have to create, curate, and distribute content tailored to your target buyer.

Put simply: give them what they want.

THUNDERBOLT IT

Like many other CEOs, Julie started each morning by cleaning out her email inbox over coffee. On this particular Thursday, she noticed an email from Bonnie with the subject line "Progress!" Intrigued, she opened it first.

It was an update on the metrics, as promised. Her email contained a report from HubSpot showing that, over the last seven days, they had converted eight website visitors into leads and received one sales opportunity that looked like a great new prospect.

She couldn't believe it. Previously, Thunderbolt IT had averaged a few leads per month at best, and practically all had come from referrals. Rarely did they get a lead from their website.

She emailed a few questions for clarification, and Bonnie responded almost immediately. She explained that by putting content offers on the website, they connected with the folks that needed information and were actively searching for help or a solution. The website traffic was always there—it was just a matter of converting some of them. Now her goal was to more proactively set up the tactics to move prospects through the Cyclonic Buyer Journey: that was the secret to driving revenue growth at Thunderbolt IT.

Julie couldn't wait to share the progress with Sam later that morning.

After working through the rest of her emails, she discovered another one from Bonnie. This one wasn't such good news. Bonnie had taken some time with Amber Lee to play "secret shoppers" with some of Thunderbolt's competitors. Their goal was to hear what stories they were telling. Unfortunately, these were almost the exact same stories that Thunderbolt IT was telling. No one stood out as different. And, based on her experience, when prospects were presented with several companies that all looked and sounded the same, they tended to choose the most inexpensive one.

Bonnie emphasized that Thunderbolt IT was not going to be thought of as a commodity on her watch. She asked Julie to join her for a messaging conversation on Monday, to get her take on how they could pull away from the rest of the pack.

Julie was a little saddened by this new insight into how poorly her company was positioned in the marketplace. She agreed to the meeting, then showered, dressed, and headed over to the Bean Café.

Sam reviewed Bonnie's plan for converting website

visitors into leads and was impressed. "Not only is this a great plan, Julie, but it has produced some early results! You are making real progress."

"I agree. It seems like it's going in the right direction, but we still don't have any new clients," she commented.

He smiled a knowing smile. "Your feelings are very normal, Julie. Almost everyone thinks leads should materialize immediately, but it doesn't work like that. You're going to have to be more patient. It took you years to get into this situation, and it's going to take you a few months to get out of it. The most successful of my engagements were the ones where the leaders were patient—very patient. Programs like the one you and Bonnie are creating take time to get traction. But once completed and optimized, they produce consistent results for years to come. Give it a few months before you start to worry. Trust me and trust Bonnie.

"So, let's talk about the next cyclone that your buyers have to navigate. Once they're aware that they need a solution, they're going to want to get educated on all the options. That's the Education stage.

"To recap, your prospects have already experienced the Pre-awareness and Awareness stages. What makes their behavior different in this stage is that they are active. They are taking action to get educated; they are proactively looking for content and information. In this stage, it's our job to help them on their educational journey. Let's create content and offers—without attempting to sell them anything, since they aren't ready to buy anyway—that will really help them understand their options. It will position Thunderbolt IT as a trusted source of information and draw them a little closer to us. That nurturing will continue to build a relationship, albeit in the background," Sam explained.

"Finally, make sure that Bonnie and Amber Lee are creating these offers with the intention of helping, not selling. Help and information are what prospects crave at this juncture in their buying journey. Make sure your educational content is in a variety of formats: videos, podcasts, infographics, white papers, e-books, slide decks, webinars, and events. You're going to want to test a variety of formats to see which ones produce the most and the highest quality leads."

When Julie returned to the office, she called Bonnie into the conference room to chat. She described the next stage Sam had discussed with her and asked Bonnie what her plans might include for educational content.

"I was already thinking of this stage," Bonnie said. "We have some of these offers, like white papers and e-books, for the Awareness cyclone, but I want to start differentiating ourselves like we discussed. My thought was to create a video university for us."

Julie arched an eyebrow. "A video university?"

"We have a unique opportunity with Thunderbolt IT. Few owners of firms like ours have a leader who likes to do public speaking, and there are practically no women in our industry. I want to create an in-house TV show each week—featuring you. We can take that room in the back (I think it was a server room before you migrated to the cloud) and, for about $1,200 in equipment, turn it into a video studio, with a set like *Late Night with David Letterman*. You'd be the host, and each week, we could plan for guests to join you, have special segments on hot topics, and mix in a bit of fun and creativity. Those old two- to three-minute talking-head videos that businesses create are becoming a bit passé. With the way people binge-watch their content now, we can take more of a Netflix approach.

"We'll leave the older episodes ungated but place the three most recent episodes behind a conversion form that new viewers must complete before they can see them. That will make it a bit more exclusive and help build our database of interested parties while still focusing on the education of our prospects. Then we build out a YouTube channel and tag each episode with search terms, to drive more traffic to our website. We'll also push each video out via social media, to increase our reach and repurpose our work. Finally, I'll work with Jonathan and the sales team to insert the most current video into our ongoing sales process."

Having talked herself out, she took a breath while waiting for Julie to take it all in.

"Hmmm," Julie said, "I do like the idea of creating up-to-date content that our customers and prospects can access at any time. And putting the newest three behind a gate, as you call it, to get their email address is a nice touch. Okay, this all sounds great. Let's do it!"

Bonnie's tone changed as she spoke again. "Julie, there is one other thing I want to talk about. I was looking over the data from the sales team, and then I met with Jonathan. Great guy, but as the VP of sales, I think he could be delivering more. Would you be open to me assisting them? They have no visibility into what's working and what's not. I want to help them implement HubSpot's CRM. It's free to start, and when we get it all set up, you're only looking at around $400 to $500 a month to put the six sales reps on it. It's going to give us data to make better decisions in the sales process. I'll help Jonathan set it up to match what we already have. Can I move forward on that?"

Julie replied, "Of course. But please be sensitive to the fact that Jonathan has been with our firm for nine years and has helped us get where we are. I don't want him to feel like we are bulldozing him."

"I completely understand. I've been in companies where it was sales versus marketing. That's one of the reasons I left my last job. I feel like Jonathan and I already have a good working relationship, and I respect that his team played a huge role in bringing the company to $45 million in revenue. This is one change we'll need to get us to our target of $100 million."

After Bonnie left her office, Julie reflected on what things had been like when she'd started Thunderbolt IT; the new sales and marketing model was so complex that she felt overwhelmed. But that was why she'd hired great people and encouraged them to take risks—exactly what she was doing with Bonnie.

6

THE ELIMINATION ROUND: THE CYCLONE OF CONSIDERATION

The really important question to answer is this:
Why would a person choose to do business with you at all?

—ROY H. WILLIAMS, *SECRET FORMULAS OF THE WIZARD OF ADS*

It's easier to fight the enemy you can see than the one you can't.

Companies—and by that, we mean the people who compose them—want to identify the competition and crush them. It's why they measure market share, brand awareness, stock price, and other such metrics. It's a way to tell whether they're winning or not. The customer is a prize to be won; a competitor, the dragon to be slain.

They have misidentified the enemy.

When hotels measure their market share against their competitors, they don't take Airbnb into account because it's not a hotel chain. It's not in their industry (though it is definitely on their radar). As this goes to print, Airbnb boasts more than three hundred million nights booked since its founding in August 2009. Your competitors aren't the other guys listed in your industry's trade journal. Your competition is anything that can solve the buyer's pain.

The real battle takes place in the buyer's mind. You aren't vying for their business against another industry leader. You're competing for their business against all their fears, responsibilities, hopes, distractions, tasks, emotions, and health problems. You're competing against their social norms, cultural values, self-identity, career plans, spiritual beliefs, and everything else that makes them human. You compete against the inertia—and the comfort—of changing nothing.

We live in a day and age where people often make buying choices based on whether your company aligns with their social views (especially here in the polarized political environment of the United States). Plenty of Christians eat at Chick-fil-A and shop at Hobby Lobby because they see those companies sharing their religious beliefs, refusing to frequent Starbucks for the same reason. In 2016 alone, consumers bought more than $8.7 billion worth of products through Fairtrade International, just one of several fair trade organizations. Socially responsible investing (SRI) funds that incorporate environmental, social, and governance considerations into their investments manage at least $60 trillion worth of assets.[20] People invest in SRI funds because of their performance *and* their commitment to social causes.

If you think about it, every investor chooses their portfolio based on more than just fund performance. If you run an investment management firm, the financial advisors you sell to aren't recommending your funds to their clients based on performance alone but a number of client-specific preferences. It doesn't matter how impeccable of a track record your growth fund has. A retired grandmother in Florida doesn't want to put her nest egg in a portfolio of risky tech companies.

When you're trying to influence a buyer in the Consideration cyclone, you're not just trying to get them to choose you over your competitor; you're trying to get them to choose this course of action over anything else that would keep them from moving forward.

Take Barrett Ersek, founder and CEO of Happy Lawn. (Well, former CEO; in 2009, he sold it to lawn care giant TruGreen, then went on to found plant probiotics

---

20 Principles for Responsible Investment, "Integrate the Principles for Responsible Investment," United Nations Global Compact, https://www.unglobalcompact.org /take-action/action/responsible-investment.

manufacturer Holganix.) Happy Lawn did more than cut your grass. It provided lawn aeration, insect control, fungus control, fertilization, winterizing, and more. When the company launched its new shrub and tree care protection program, it struggled to get people to sign up—notably, its current lawn care customers.

This was particularly perplexing. Barrett and the rest of the executive team knew customers raved about their services. One testimonial they liked to frequently refer to read: "Your service is terrific! You guys beat the snot out of your competition!" Obviously, their customers knew, liked, and trusted Happy Lawn. In their minds, at least, they weren't competing against other companies' shrubbery care services.

The Happy Lawn leadership team knew other companies in similar markets had successfully provided the same service for years. It wasn't as if they were rolling out a revolutionary new idea in uncharted territory; the customers for this service existed. Thinking price might be the issue, marketing rolled out a discounted monthly subscription plan: $39 a month. Still nothing.

The team was understandably frustrated. The margin on adding this service to existing contracts was quite high. That fact coupled with the volume Happy Lawn did as one of the largest lawn care companies in the Mid-Atlantic meant it was leaving a serious amount of potential revenue on the table. So much so that the leadership team hired our agency just for this specific challenge.

After a small phone survey, we discovered that customers didn't really care about the cost of the service. Some thought it a touch high or a touch low. Most thought it was reasonable. We did, however, discover what they were terrified of: the cost of replacing all of their trees and bushes.

We repositioned Happy Lawn's message. Instead of focusing on the value of $39 a month, we told the story of a homeowner who'd spent $14,896 to replace his trees after a particularly harsh winter: "If only he'd had Happy Lawn's new Shrub and Tree Protection Program!"

Day One of the new promotion saw forty-two customers subscribe.

Looking at this situation through the lens of the buyer's cyclone, Happy Lawn's prospective subscribers were in the Awareness cyclone. They knew a problem existed (the potential loss of trees and shrubs to disease or weather), but they didn't have enough pain to do anything about it. Happy Lawn's new campaign drove their anxiety of loss high enough that they took immediate action.

While this story is really about influencing a buyer in the Awareness cyclone, we include it here because it's such a poignant example of how even when you don't have competition . . . you still have competition. Even when you think you're the obvious choice, your customers have options. It was only by understanding how their current (!) customers saw not just the company but *this* particular service that Happy Lawn began to see the serious additional revenue Barrett knew was possible.

Competing Against Nothing: Influencing Done Right

Let's look at a conventional example of a buyer in the cyclone of Consideration.

Drucker & Scaccetti provides tax and accounting services to entrepreneurs, business owners, and high-net-worth people. It specializes in complex tax situations and using tax as a business strategy for CEOs who want to protect their hard-earned income. The type of clients the firm wanted already had an accountant. To grow, Drucker & Scaccetti faced the option of going head-to-head with someone's entrenched, trusted advisor who had brought them this far or going after smaller fish to get in earlier and eventually become that entrenched, trusted advisor. Neither was a particularly appealing option.

How do you influence someone to consider other options? How do you get someone to know other options might actually be better for them, even when they're happy with their current provider?

We suggested that the firm needed to trigger its target clients' pain by sowing doubt about the competition's capabilities. If you're like us, you begrudge every penny you pay Uncle Sam. We firmly believe in the words of federal judge Learned Hand[21] who once wrote, "Any one may so arrange his affairs so that his taxes shall be as low as possible; he is not bound to choose that pattern which

---

21   Yes, that's really his name.

will best pay the Treasury,"[22] and then later, "Everybody does so, rich or poor, and all do right, for nobody owes any public duty to pay more than the law demands."[23]

Wealthy people paying a lot in taxes are always worried that they're paying too much. In that regard, they perpetually live in the Awareness cyclone; they get a reminder every week when their paycheck shows how much went to the U.S. Treasury. Even when you're outwardly happy with your tax advisors, no matter how much you trust them, you always wonder if there was a way you could have paid less. The more money you make, the more you wonder.

That's the mindset we keyed in on with Drucker & Scaccetti. The firm needed to get its target audience questioning their current situation: *Am I paying too much in taxes? These guys specialize in working with people like me. My accountant's good, but are these guys better? They do specialize in working with people like me, after all.* And around and around their thoughts would go.

Playing to those fears triggered their pain, often resulting in them spinning right into the Consideration cyclone. Once there, they generally had three options: talk to Drucker & Scaccetti, take the initiative to find other tax accountants, or stay with their current accountant.

---

22 Helvering v. Gregory, 69 F.2d 809, 810 (2d Cir. 1934), https://law.justia.com/cases/federal/appellate-courts/F2/69/809/1562063/.

23 Commissioner of Internal Revenue v. Newman, 159 F.2d 848 (2d Cir. 1947), https://law.justia.com/cases/federal/appellate-courts/F2/159/848/1565902/.

It's crucial that you key in on the importance of that. The following tactics to influence business owners and professionals don't work in isolation. If a tech entrepreneur saw an email with the subject line "Drucker & Scaccetti, specializing in tax—," they wouldn't even finish reading before deleting. If a sales rep somehow managed to get them on the phone, the entrepreneur would say, "No thanks, I'm happy with my current provider, goodbye" before the salesperson could open their mouth. These tactics would bounce off their mental shield of "things I don't need to worry about today." Only because Drucker & Scaccetti's previous tactics triggered their pain and got them to start rethinking their options did the following stand a chance.

John Jantsch wrote in *Duct Tape Marketing* that people only do business with people they know, like, and trust. Put another way: people only make purchasing decisions when they feel safe, and if you want someone to feel safe, they need to know, like, and trust you. This has been at the cornerstone of the psychology of buyer behavior for decades. With a prospective buyer in the Consideration cyclone worried about paying too much in taxes, we needed to give them opportunities to get to know the firm, like the people, and trust their expertise. We accomplished that by simply creating a steady stream of educational content, social media posts, in-office events, and opportunities for the prospective clients to get to know the tax experts. Once this evolved from a "when we can get to it" activity into a regular cadence of strategic, planned, and well-executed marketing touches, the prospects followed.

That was it.

From the outside looking in, it doesn't look like Drucker & Scaccetti did anything differently than any of the dozens of other accounting firms competing in the same space. It didn't. The difference was that it didn't use sales tactics to try to bully a busy executive into taking a meeting. It found a way to influence buyers in the Awareness cyclone, agitate their fears so that they found themselves in the Consideration cyclone, then presented them with a number of opportunities to get to know, like, and trust the firm's experts. Drucker & Scaccetti took the long view, patiently executed a well-orchestrated plan, and reaped the reward of highly qualified leads.

From there, the sale itself happened almost effortlessly.

From "One of Many" to "One of Few"

Now that your buyer has settled on a course of action (that was the whole influencing goal in the cyclone of Education), they're considering all the possible providers of that course of action. You're just one of many.

Think about the reality show *The Bachelor*. (We know, we know, but just stay with us for a minute.) At the start of the series, said bachelor has about two dozen women hand-picked by the producers of the show, all of whom want to become "the one." Over the course of the next eleven weeks, he continually ranks them until he's narrowed it down to just a handful.

While we in no way suggest you take any life lessons from reality TV, you absolutely should take some business lessons. In wooing the bachelor, the contestants aren't trying to win his undying love in the beginning. Nor do they need to. They just need to survive the elimination rounds by standing out and making a connection.

THUNDERBOLT IT

Julie met Bonnie on Monday to discuss how to differentiate Thunderbolt IT from the competition. Bonnie had also asked Jonathan to sit in on the meeting, since he and his sales team interacted directly with buyers daily.

Bonnie started by asking them to identify the key personas (or profiles) of the people involved in a purchasing decision for Thunderbolt's services. Julie was surprised that Jonathan listed four separate personas. He identified the CIO, who was the primary buyer; the CFO was often involved, since it was a sizable financial investment; the COO was an influencer, since the software had a direct impact on operations; and in most cases the CEO was also involved. In a few of the most recent wins, purchasing was also involved: usually a purchasing manager. Jonathan mentioned that it would really be great if he had more sales collateral for all four personas, since they only had materials that were created for the CIO.

They then discussed how the pain points were different, depending on the decision-maker's role. They also talked about how those pain points sometimes shifted, depending on where the decision-maker was in their buyer journey. In the Awareness stage, potential buyers were less educated about what an IT services provider could do for a business. As they moved through their journey and became more educated, they would start to see everything that Thunderbolt could offer them. But what all four personas had in common was that they were trying to meet the same overall challenge: operational efficiency, which included cost reduction and employee optimization. Historically, whether a client sold widgets or provided professional services, they bought from Thunderbolt IT in order to reach business outcomes more quickly and effectively.

Bonnie asked, "Which industry do we usually do the best in?"

Julie stated that they could help any business but that they tended to do better in two specific areas: financial services and manufacturing. They discussed that since they had two mammoth clients in financial services already, they should start to diversify by targeting more manufacturing accounts.

"As the newcomer to Thunderbolt," Bonnie replied, "I'll raise my hand to ask the obvious: why would a manufacturer choose us over the competition?"

Julie explained that the roots of their services went deep into building process improvements for manufacturers.

"The way we approach our solutions for clients is from an engineering lens, so our legacy and expertise both support manufacturing firms. Basically, we speak their language!"

"But how do we help them achieve operational efficiency, as you call it?" Bonnie asked.

Julie described three ways they helped:

- First, they had a five-step process they used to cocreate and design a new client's IT solution.

- Second, they created a team of engineers and coders that could respond to client issues at any time of the day. No matter what the problem, this team could respond and get it fixed in minutes.

- Third, for custom software development projects, the company circled back with each client every ninety days, both to check on the integrity of the software and to verify that the original business objectives were being realized.

"This is amazing! Why didn't I read about any of this stuff on the website?" Bonnie blurted out.

"We are much better IT experts than storytellers, I guess," replied Jonathan.

Over the next few days, Bonnie developed three specific differentiators based on the programs Julie described, including—

- The 5 D's™ Development Process: Discovery, Diagnostic, Design, Delivery, Delight
- The Rapid Response Team™
- The 90-Day CircleBack Program™

Bonnie now had enough ammunition to help prospects in the Education stage see that Thunderbolt IT was remarkable—to see that they were different than the other IT providers—and to emotionally connect with them so that they would want to learn more.

Julie reminded them that after the Education stage, prospects entered the Consideration stage and began looking at options. "They've decided to do *something* but are still evaluating exactly what. They might hire in-house; they might hire an outside provider. They're not sure yet—but they know they're taking some action!"

To help with prospects in the Consideration stage, Bonnie asked Amber Lee to work on some content to target people at this stage:

- a white paper discussing the ways manufacturers could improve their operational efficiency, including building their own software, offshoring the process, or hiring a consultant like Thunderbolt IT (this would help prospects understand their options while subtly pointing to the fact that hiring Thunderbolt was the best option);

- a video case study of an existing client who went through the selection process and developed a solution together with the Thunderbolt IT team (this would help prospective clients identify with other companies in the same situation); and

- a webinar success story with that same client, which could also be repurposed for use in another format.

The three executives felt they had the story and the delivery tactics needed to differentiate Thunderbolt IT from its competitors—specifically for someone considering a project to help them improve their manufacturing.

Just to make sure they had enough firepower behind the effort, Bonnie created a new paid social campaign in order to test the new offers and messaging and to get some data on what people connected with. She used LinkedIn and selected only the COOs of manufacturers with over $100 million in revenue and 250 or more employees.

Then they waited for the numbers to come in.

7

THE CHOSEN FEW: THE CYCLONE OF EVALUATION

Before him he saw two roads, both equally straight; but he did see two; and that terrified him—he who had never in his life known anything but one straight line. And, bitter anguish, these two roads were contradictory.

—VICTOR HUGO, *LES MISÉRABLES*

This is where you get to say you're "better than the other guys."

This chapter should feel familiar; it's what the vast majority of sales and marketing efforts today revolve around. In the lingo of the sales funnel, "These guys are thinking about hiring us! Holy mackerel, Batman—how do we get them to the bottom of the funnel!?"

It's where you get to brag about how much better your products and services are and how much your customers love you. It's the field of battle where you duke it out with your archrivals and the winner gets to kiss the customer. At least, that's how most people see it.

This is also where most companies blow it.

Let's say you're in the grocery store and decide you want to try some new cereal. It's easy to quickly eliminate most options. Wanting to be a little healthier, you ignore the sugary oldie but goodies of your childhood and examine the "adult" cereals. You do, however, want a little taste, so that takes plain Special K and others like it out of the mix. You don't care for the taste of chocolate, you don't like nuts, and you're allergic to cinnamon. Eliminating those cereals (i.e., considering all of your potential options) takes a matter of seconds. You spend the next fifteen minutes ranking the remaining choices (i.e., seriously evaluating a few options) as if the fate of the world rested on your breakfast choice of Special K Red Berries, Very Berry Cheerios, or Cheerios + Ancient Grains.

When your buyer is in the Consideration cyclone, they compare you to all of the other potential ways to execute the course of action they decided on in the previous cyclone of educating and informing themselves. When your buyer is in the Evaluation cyclone, they have pared down their potential options to a select few.

In the previous example of the tax accounting firm Drucker & Scaccetti, its buyers already had accountants;

the only two paths most of its clients even thought about were whether to stay with their existing firm or switch. When prospects make the decision to change firms, however, they're not going to evaluate just one new firm; they're going to evaluate a few, "just to be sure." The game is different in this stage.

When you do find your buyer evaluating just a few options, what do you do?

One of Few to the Obvious Choice

Take the case of SynaTek Solutions.

The business sold liquid turf fertilizer primarily to golf courses, who, in turn, injected the product into their irrigation systems. The industry norm had been to sell the required pumping equipment to the golf courses and then sell the liquid fertilizer on an ongoing basis to the superintendents of the courses, thereby creating a steady and recurring revenue stream. This presented several problems for SynaTek when it came on the business scene:

- Getting golf course management committees to approve the large expenditure of buying pumping equipment was a long, arduous, and uphill process.

- The fertilizers each company sold were basically commodities; there wasn't anything particularly special or notable about one company's over another's.

- Even after buying the pumping equipment from one vendor, nothing prevented the superintendents from switching to a cheaper competitor. This severely limited the recurring revenue play and put a big dent in companies' revenue growth plans.

SynaTek could have taken the traditional approach and tried to compete on the field of battle against other fertilizer companies, railing about how underhanded and shady its competitors were and how great its fertilizer was, and "Hey, how ya doin', here's a special discount just for you."

Instead, SynaTek took the smarter approach: it got into the minds of its buyers. In this case, as is the case with most B2B buying decisions, "buyers" comprised a number of people: the golf course superintendent plus the members of the committee managing the course. In the *Harvard Business Review* article "The New Sales Imperative," the authors reported that the number involved in a B2B decision averaged 5.4 people in 2015; by 2017, it had risen to 6.8. [24]

From the perspective of the committee managers, they didn't want to spend extra money on pumping equipment just so the vendor could sell them even more products. From the perspective of the superintendent, he (virtually

---

24 Nicholas Toman, Brent Adamson, and Cristina Gomez, "The New Sales Imperative," *Harvard Business Review*, March–April 2017, https://hbr.org/2017/03/the-new-sales-imperative.

always a male) didn't want to fight with the committee to get them to approve the additional expenditure. He wanted to run his golf course smoothly and keep it beautiful.

Well, reasoned SynaTek, if buying the equipment is the big problem, why not take that out of the equation? The company decided to offer golf courses the equipment for free. What had been a major revenue source for turf fertilizer companies was suddenly the price of admission for the industry! The catch was that the golf courses had to sign a multiyear agreement to buy fertilizer from SynaTek.

What a brilliant play.

The superintendents loved the arrangement because they wouldn't have to fight with management, and what the hell, they already had turf fertilizer in the budget! The golf course managers might have loved it, but most didn't know anything about it because the new approach completely circumvented them. SynaTek loved it because the deal instantly made the company far and away its customers' best option, allowed it to sell fertilizer at top dollar, guaranteed a stream of revenue that wouldn't be subject to competition for years to come, and left other providers scrambling to catch up.

Let's look at this story through the lens of the buyer's cyclonic journey. First, SynaTek had no problems with its buyer getting stuck in the Education cyclone. While buying weed and feed from Lowe's in bulk and fertilizing by hand was technically an option, these are major golf courses we're talking about here—anything less than professional grade doesn't cut it.

Nor did SynaTek have a problem with a buyer getting stuck in the Consideration cyclone. While its market was highly competitive, there were only a handful of professional turf fertilizer suppliers. It was "one of few" by default. Its problem was figuring out how to stand out among those vendors—how to become "remarkable."

Next, SynaTek's approach found a way to take a "buyer" from being composed of several people to a single person. It's always easier to influence an individual than a whole committee. (How many deals has your own company lost because HR, legal, or accounting raised a red flag, overriding your primary contact's wishes?)

This also achieved the major goal for influencing buyers in the Evaluation cyclone: it made the company the obvious choice. SynaTek's magic bullet solution made it so easy for the golf course superintendent that it was harder for him to say no than to say yes.

Stroke of genius.

Turning $250 into $250,000

But what if you could get your buyer to skip this cyclone altogether?

Cue Rittenhouse Builders.

One challenge virtually every company has is knowing exactly who they're selling to. We've said for years how easy our jobs would be if all of our clients wanted to "sell mozzarella to Philly pizzerias"—someone who knew precisely what they're selling to whom. In *Fire Your Sales Team Today,* we wrote about Springboard Media, a multilocation Apple retail partner.

> When they opened their next store, the marketing team came to us with a two-page list of all the possible advertising options they could use to promote the grand opening. *Whoa,* we thought, *they can't all be right for this type of store!*
>
> . . . When we challenged them to picture the perfect buyer, they described an affluent mom or dad living within five miles of the store who appreciates great service, needs training on Apple products, and loves accessories to go with his or her new computer. They described these buyers as "driving up in their Range Rovers to attend a training class with their kids." We named the Springboard Media avatar Jen.
>
> "Would Jen respond to coupons in the local penny pincher?" we asked.
>
> "Probably not," they confirmed.
>
> We proceeded to go through the list of promotional options and crossed off more than half, each time asking, "Would Jen respond to this?"

If you're a marketing professional, this should be elementary, but we still see $100 million companies struggling to understand how to apply this persona-centric approach to their marketing tactics. For the CEO at Springboard Media, this was an eye-opening exercise. It helped him picture exactly who his company was trying to influence at which stage of their journey.

This was not Rittenhouse Builders' problem. It knew exactly who it was looking for: homeowners of $2 million houses in a specific geography looking to do a $250,000 addition or remodel. *That's* selling mozzarella to Philly pizzerias.

Like SynaTek, though, Rittenhouse faced fierce competition, even in the market for high-end, luxury home construction and remodeling. Some of its prospective buyers stayed whirling around in the Consideration cyclone, overwhelmed by all the contractors available. The rest whirled around the Evaluation cyclone, trying to figure out which three or four contractors were best—all of whom claimed to do excellent work, had portfolios of beautiful before-and-after pictures, and had a gazillion satisfied customer testimonials. Often, it came down to some minor detail, a gut feeling, or which one they liked most.

We are quite proud of the solution. It sidestepped the Evaluation cyclone altogether. We worked with them to develop a program called Rittenhouse Express, a professional handyman service tucked inside Rittenhouse Builders' traditional business. For just $249 for a half day, you got a Rittenhouse Craftsman to handle your honey-do list. This echoes Enterprise Financial Consulting's tack of offering free webinars to CFOs. On the surface, "one-man handyman" jobs were not the market Rittenhouse wanted to be in. The builder did quarter-of-a-million-dollar remodels, for crying out loud; $249 was peanuts. That's the equivalent of hiring Deloitte to do your personal income taxes, the proverbial "cannon to kill a mosquito."

You already see where this is going.

Of *course* the homeowners loved it. Of *course* the Rittenhouse Craftsman made a great impression. Of *course* they talked about the bigger project the homeowner would love to do "someday." Of *course* many contracted Rittenhouse Express for additional days and projects. Of *course* plenty of those customers quickly opted for the bigger remodel and many of the rest followed suit soon after. Of *course* Rittenhouse Express quickly became the company's best source of leads for $250,000 remodels and additions.

Of course.

In fact, the handyman service not only succeeded, it exploded to the point Rittenhouse spun it off into its own company. The referrals from it grew the core business by ten times, even during some very lean years.

On paper, this looks so logical and easy. Why, then, don't more companies look for these kinds of opportunities? Ironically, the companies in the best position to risk something like this—enterprise-level businesses—give us the most grief about proposed ideas along these lines. The companies least able to roll the dice and take the potential financial hit—small businesses—have often been the most willing to try something new. The success of Rittenhouse Express turning into a steady stream of people ready to take out a second mortgage for a home addition stems from the fact that, instead of going head-to-head against other high-end contractors in the Evaluation and Consideration cyclones, Rittenhouse found its buyers when they were in their Awareness cyclones . . . and then addressed an entirely different problem.

This accomplished two things.

One, it established a wonderful relationship with the target market. When homeowners were ready to do the big project, they skipped the Education, Consideration, and Evaluation cyclones. They already knew, liked, and trusted Rittenhouse; why would they even think about using someone else?

Two, it agitated their desire so that instead of being stuck in the Awareness cyclone, daydreaming "*I'd love to do that addition someday . . .*" they were ready to start learning about how to fulfill that desire: "Just curious, if we *were* thinking about adding on, do you know how much it would be?"

The Remarkable Choice

Even here, you're still not trying to get your buyer to buy.

You simply want to influence them so that they see you as the obvious choice.

If they simply see you as the best choice, you haven't

done your job. You want to stand out so far that you stand apart altogether. Rittenhouse wasn't the best choice in its buyers' minds—it was the *obvious* choice. The same for Enterprise Financial Consulting and SynaTek. To their buyers, they became, in effect, a category of one. It's like comparing apples to apples, then finding a ruby in the basket—it's not even in the same league.

Take a look at Texas-based commercial beverage supplier Red River Tea. When it wanted to expand its flagship product Teazzers from a regional market to a national one, it knew it'd be competing head-on with the likes of FUZE, Gold Peak, and AriZona in the convenience store segment and Lipton and Luzianne, among others, in the restaurant segment.

When we revamped their branding, the goal wasn't to directly convince the restaurateurs and convenience store owners to buy Teazzers. We wanted them to give Teazzers a try. Or, from the frame of cyclonic marketing, we wanted Teazzers to go from being seen as one of dozens and dozens of iced-tea suppliers to one of their top choices. Their not-from-concentrate, fresh-brewed taste truly is remarkable.

That's your goal: to be the remarkable choice.

THUNDERBOLT IT

Sam listened intently while Julie excitedly explained all of the recent sales and marketing improvements her team had made since they last met.

"Julie," he began, "I think we should suspend our next few sessions."

She was shocked.

"But I'm doing exactly what you recommended. I've kept to all three of your conditions," she reminded him.

"Yes! In fact, you are progressing so well, I suggest you use the time we meet to help Bonnie and Jonathan instead. The next few stages are when they are really going to need you to help them create a remarkable experience for your prospects.

"You see, Julie, Thunderbolt IT is now ready to attack the Evaluation cyclone. In this stage, prospects have made a decision. They've decided that they're not doing it themselves, they're going to hire someone—and they've even narrowed down their choices. This is big. They've decided to go with a firm like yours, but now you have to beat out a handful of other firms to get the work. This is where differentiation and experience in the sales process is key, and I think you, Bonnie, and Jonathan should work on this together. At this stage, buyers need even more highly relevant content to help them decide between all of the possible firms. In all my research, I have found that this is the critical time, the stage where most clients will select you or your competition. I want you to focus on Evaluation and the processes that go with it until they are built and fine-tuned."

Julie was relieved. "I thought you were firing me!" After a laugh, she said, "All right, so when should we schedule our next coffee? A month?"

"I think you're going to have your hands full, Julie. Let's say sixty days."

When she got back to Thunderbolt, Julie buzzed Bonnie and Jonathan and asked them to come into her office. She explained to them what Sam had encouraged them to do and shared her ideas for the Evaluation stage.

Jonathan said, "Sam is right. We really need your help. Bonnie and I have redesigned our sales process to help buyers progress through the cyclones he described. But no matter how we rework it, we need it to be better."

Bonnie added, "Amber Lee and I have created content that I think speaks to people in this stage. We wrote an e-book called *Nine Questions to Ask Your Software Development Partner Before You Hire Them*. On top of that, our latest videos are designed to be used by sales when prospects reach out to us. We're focusing the video content on our differentiators, what makes Thunderbolt IT remarkable. This should help us tell our story and clearly stand apart from any competitors. We also asked our new Rapid Response Team to develop another five case studies showcasing our work. But we feel it's not enough."

Over the last eight weeks or so, Bonnie's new marketing efforts had produced a good selection of qualified sales opportunities, but they hadn't closed any new customers worth talking about. They started looking to the sales process as the next place for improvements. Their HubSpot CRM produced some reports that showed that prospects were getting stuck. In order to produce a higher close rate, they needed a set of upgrades to make the process tighter and more remarkable; what they were already doing was not producing the expected or desired results.

When they looked at the data, they realized very few prospects were asking for references, and they were not getting to provide pricing and investment analysis to prospects. The sales process was stalling out early. Bonnie and Jonathan viewed this as an indication that Thunderbolt IT was not making it into the group of firms that prospects were comparing. Understanding how their prospects liked to receive their information, Bonnie leaned on creating two additional offers.

First, the sales team was going to reach out to any sales-qualified leads (SQLs) in manufacturing and offer them a systems analysis at no charge, one hundred percent complimentary. The client services team would work directly with sales to do a quick review of the prospect's current configuration and make some high-level recommendations. This would introduce the prospect to the people they'd be working with if they became clients *and* give them real value for their business as part of the sales process. Amber Lee created a website form to collect key pieces of information and metrics that the client services team would need to evaluate the prospect's current state.

In addition, Bonnie set up a lead scoring model, which would help sales focus this type of effort *only* on highly qualified prospects with a lead score above one hundred. The model also attempted, based on the prospect's online behavior, to assess the buyer journey stage and only offer the free analysis to prospects in the Evaluation stage or beyond. They all agreed that a session with the client services team was much more intimate than the "request a quote" strategy their competitors used. Additionally, Bonnie directed Amber Lee to have their video person plan for a session with Julie, to record a series of videos answering the question "Why Thunderbolt IT?"

"With these videos, we can introduce Julie to the prospects in a scalable way. This makes the buying experience more personal, gives Julie's thought leadership and experience some airtime, and positions Thunderbolt as more remarkable," Bonnie concluded.

With the 5 D's, the Rapid Response Team, and the

90-Day CircleBack Program, the Thunderbolt IT sales and marketing teams now had much better stories to tell. And by sprinkling these stories strategically throughout the marketing and sales processes, these teams had the strategies and tactics needed to not only hit but also exceed their goals.

Finally, Thunderbolt needed some online reviews. Modern prospects checked online before they even started a sales conversation, and all Thunderbolt had was one negative review from a disgruntled customer, posted three years ago. Jonathan was tasked with getting together at least a dozen five-out-of-five reviews online so that if and when prospects looked for reviews, there were plenty of positive ones.

8

"NOW I KNOW I HAD A GOOD REASON . . .": THE CYCLONE OF RATIONALIZATION

A man generally has two reasons for doing a thing:
one that sounds good, and a real one.

—J. P. MORGAN

They've decided to buy.

Now they need to figure out why.

Psychologist Daniel Kahneman won the 2002 Nobel Prize in Economic Sciences for his research (distilled and published in the 2011 *New York Times* best-selling book *Thinking, Fast and Slow*) that gave serious credence to something marketers have known for decades: human beings make subconscious, emotional decisions first and then look for information or reasons to justify those decisions at a conscious level second.

Sometimes that is to our detriment, such as making a snap judgment about a person only to later find out we were completely wrong about them or making an impulse buy that comes with its own gilded case of buyer's remorse. But as *Thinking, Fast and Slow* demonstrates, we have to make most of our decisions at a subconscious level by sheer necessity. Depending on which study you look at and how you define it, some scientists suggest that our brain processes more than two million bits of information per second. Of this, our conscious mind processes fewer than a hundred bits per second. Our subconscious has to handle the other 1,999,900-plus.

Translating that into business marketing means the shorter your buyer's journey, the more important it is that you get everything right. KPMG data shows that for most online purchases the sales cycle from Awareness to Purchase happens within a week for more than two-thirds of buyers.[25] If you're in a complex B2B sales process that takes place over a matter of months or even years, you may get by with not having a seamless, perfect buyer journey. If, on the other hand, you sell cheap smartphone cases

---

25 KPMG, "The Truth About Online Consumers," KPMG, 2017, https://home.kpmg .com/xx/en/home/insights/2017/01/the-truth-about-online-consumers.html.

online, your buyer could go from Awareness to Purchase in a matter of minutes. If they go through Amazon and have their one-click option turned on, their buying journey could happen in less than sixty seconds. In all cases, however, your buyer needs to justify their decision.

Tell them why they're making the right choice.

Why They Buy

In the Rationalization cyclone, you compete with yourself.

You've gone from "one of many" to "one of few" to "the one." When they have other explicit options to compare you to, your buyer focuses on how you stack up against other providers. When they have nothing to compare you to, it's easier for doubt to creep in. *Am I making the right choice? Is this the absolute best option? Could I find something better if I kept looking? Is it really worth the cost?*

Here, you have four focal points:

1. Remind buyers how it will feel once their pain is satisfied and removed; appeal to their emotions.

2. Make sure you know what their internal rationale checklist looks like and that you're actively working to resolve any concerns.

3. Be honest and explicit about whatever you can't solve; set their expectations.

4. Under-promise and over-deliver.

Take DVL Group, a company that primarily provides data center infrastructure. The whole idea of a data storage center revolves around risk management, stability, and security. It's easy to imagine just how careful, meticulous, and risk-averse a data center manager would be. Even if you've successfully become the obvious vendor for them, you still have a lot of work to do before they'll let you or your products into their facility and mess with anything that could even remotely jeopardize operations.

DVL's competitors act like most companies: focused on getting the sale as quickly as possible so they can hurry up and get to the next one. They are pure order-takers. You tell them what you need, they work up a quote, and then they use aggressive sales tactics to strong-arm you into signing. Because most customers don't sign, they see their industry as a numbers game and work on volume.

In contrast, DVL data center engineers spend a surprising amount of time (surprising, at least, to their customers used to dealing with pushy salespeople) walking through each and every aspect of the proposed IT solution. Another surprising delight is that "data center engineer" isn't a fancy title for their sales reps. Each is actually a trained and certified engineer. They connect with their buyers because they're more like them than they are a salesperson.

Because of this time investment, DVL's customers have already had many of their fears addressed before even coming to the Rationalization cyclone—one of the main reasons DVL became the obvious choice in the first place.

Even then, the engineers invest more time, going over integration and design specs, understanding the data center's business plan to ensure DVL's solution supports that growth instead of hindering it, and setting up detailed work schedules to avoid interfering with operations or the center's respective customers coming on-site. They are endlessly patient, addressing each and every minute detail, worry, or concern. Not only does this explicitly address the customer's fears, it implicitly says, "We're available. We want to help. We know our stuff. We want a relationship. We plan to stick around." It helps the buyer feel that, even if something does come up, they're not going to have to deal with it alone.

For a manager rationalizing their decision to use DVL, this is pure gold.

Speaking of the fear of buyer's remorse, there's an intriguing report by sales researcher Steve W. Martin wherein he conducted a survey of 230 B2B buyers from a representative cross section of industries, functions, and demographics.[26] Of particular interest is the last topic addressed; labeled as "buyer's regret," it is one of the comparatively few credible data sources we've seen on the subject in a B2B setting. Martin points out that for the survey participants expressing significant buyer's regret, seventy

---

26   Katie Bullard, "What Do B2B Buyers Want?" DiscoverOrg, https://discoverorg.com /blog/what-b2b-buyers-want/. Highlights the study "Why Didn't They Buy: A Deep Dive into Buyer Preferences and the Implications for Salespeople," researched and written by Steve W. Martin and sponsored by DiscoverOrg.

percent of the time neither the product nor the salesperson was to blame; the buyers blamed themselves, citing the following reasons, among others:

- Bought more than needed: thirteen percent
- Bought less than needed: thirteen percent
- Didn't do enough research during sales cycle: eleven percent
- Didn't negotiate the best price/discovered a price decrease: nine percent
- Focused on the short term at the cost of the long term: eight percent
- External deadline/pressure: seven percent

When a DVL data center engineer sits down with a prospect, they don't just want to make the sale; they want to ensure that the client will be satisfied with their decision over the lifetime of their relationship. They invest the time beforehand to ensure there's no buyer's remorse, regardless of the source.

Here's something else DVL's customers love: if a data center engineer doesn't have the answer, they'll go find it. If the customer wants something DVL can't deliver, they don't pretend they can. If there is some kind of unavoidable risk, not only does DVL not gloss over it, they even bring it up themselves. When was the last time a salesperson *told you* what your objections should be?

Instant credibility.

Compare this to most of the sales presentations you've sat through or marketing material you've read. They always talk about the upside, never about the downside. They worry that if they bring up a risk, you might suddenly have a worry you didn't have before. It's "let sleeping dogs lie" and "if it ain't broke, don't fix it." That mentality simply doesn't fly today. DVL's buyer is an extremely capable person. You don't get hired to manage a data center serving millions of customers because you want a low-key job with weekends and holidays off. Trying to pull the wool over these managers' eyes doesn't work. They're too smart for that.

What's more, that's not just the case for DVL's buyer— that's the reality of every customer today. It's the whole reason the sales funnel doesn't work anymore. Consumers don't call the Better Business Bureau to see if you've had any complaints; they just go online to some review site or see how many Amazon stars you have. Pretending that an obvious problem doesn't exist is like hiding behind a lamppost. It's funny when a child does it but concerning when it's an adult.

Addressing your buyer's objections before they even raise them earns you their trust. Addressing an issue that your product or service can't solve earns you their admiration, especially if you beat them to the punch. It is lamentable that such honesty is noteworthy, but because it is, you can use it to your advantage.

How B2B Tech Buyers Rationalize a Purchase

In 2017 tech research firm TrustRadius conducted a survey to examine "the gaps between how B2B buyers make purchasing decisions and how B2B vendors influence them."[27] Their findings are fascinating (at least, to business nerds like us) to the point we could spend an entire chapter dissecting the findings.

To convince you of the broad applicability of the information we're about to present, look at a partial view of the surveyed buyers:

- Size of buyer company
    - 1–10 employees, nine percent
    - 1,001–5,000 employees, fifteen percent
    - 10,001-plus employees, seven percent

- Department of buyer
    - IT, thirty-one percent
    - marketing, twenty-seven percent
    - accounting and finance, seven percent
    - engineering, four percent

- Type of software purchased
    - IT, sixteen percent
    - marketing automation, fifteen percent

27   Vala Afshar, "The B2B Buying Disconnect," Huffington Post, February 8, 2017, https://www.huffingtonpost.com/entry/the-b2b-buying-disconnect _us_589b53dce4b0985224db5cb9. Refers to the 2017 B2B Buying Disconnect study published by TrustRadius.

- CRM, ten percent
- business intelligence, nine percent
- other, twenty-two percent

The point here is that this was a wide-ranging survey, representing everything from solopreneurs automating their social media to enterprise-level executives buying enterprise resource planning (ERP) software.

What did TrustRadius find?

Buyers said the most helpful source of information was a free trial or account; second, a product demo; third, a peer referral; fourth, user reviews. Sales reps and their presentations tied for fifth place with customer references. Out of twelve possible information sources, the least helpful was the vendor's website; second least, vendor collateral.

Let's look at that. Of the top five best sources of product information, four of them didn't involve vendor interaction at all. (It's almost as if buyers have taken companies' selling process out of their hands altogether.) The worst sources were the seller's website and traditional marketing collateral. Yet that's precisely where companies spend so much of their marketing budget because, well, "We have to have a pretty website!"

In another question, TrustRadius asked buyers to rank the trustworthiness of information sources. Unsurprisingly, their answers align with what they found helpful. The least trusted source was vendor collateral, then the vendor's website, then the sales rep and their presentations.

Our number one takeaway from this insightful survey was that your buyer doesn't want to hear from you and won't trust you when they do. They want validation from sources you don't control: peer referrals, user reviews, customer references, third-party recommendations, analysts, third-party publications, and so forth.

Let's look at this from the perspective of the Rationalization cyclone. When your buyer is trying to justify choosing you, the best way to influence them is by letting your buyer convince themselves.

Give them the opportunity to try your product or service, like the "freemium" model of many tech startups or Zappos's legendary return policy. Take screenshots of five-star user reviews of your product or service on third-party sites or share the links. Get enthusiastic customers to record a testimonial from their phone or laptop to post to YouTube. Have a list of loyal clients and customers willing to share their email address or even phone number to act as a reference.

The number one recommendation by TrustRadius? B2B tech vendors should invest serious time, energy, and money into creating a customer referral program:

> Vendors aren't fully leveraging [their] customers. Though 46% of buyers are by definition promoters and 42% have recommended the product directly to a peer, most have not taken any action on behalf of the vendor to promote the product. Overall, just 20% of

buyers said they took [action]. . . . This represents a missed opportunity for vendors, who have **an arsenal of satisfied customers not speaking on their behalf** in a way that can reach prospects at scale.[28]

When a Sales Rep Can't Be Present

The TrustRadius survey includes products bought absent any interaction with a salesperson, but when you think of B2B tech sales, you usually picture a sales guy giving a presentation in a conference room. So let's dig down for a moment to think about products and industries where you wouldn't have a salesperson there.

Reach back to our cereal example from earlier. Out of all the cereals you could have chosen, you quickly homed in on the three that fit your criteria: Special K Red Berries, Very Berry Cheerios, and Cheerios + Ancient Grains. After evaluating, you decide that "Ancient Grains" sounds so . . . cool. Into your basket it goes. You pick up the rest of your grocery list and head to the checkout.

While standing in line, you start thinking that "Ancient Grains" actually sounds . . . well, a little weird. You wanted an adult cereal, not an adventurous one. When it's your turn to check out, you set the box aside. Maybe next time you'll stick with something a little less dramatic. And didn't the Special K Red Berries have the Susan G. Komen logo

---

28   Emphasis added.

on it? Eat well and do good! Maybe that's what you'll get. Next time.

You were in the cyclone of Rationalization. You had picked out one cereal and carried it all the way to the point of purchase—and changed your mind at the last minute, reverting back to the cyclone of Evaluation. Depending on your mood the next time you go grocery shopping, you might even revert back to the cyclone of Consideration.

We have no doubt that you've done the same thing online; abandoned shopping carts are usually online retailers' biggest frustration, standing at about sixty-nine percent across the board.[29] With such buyers, understanding their reasoning is a little murkier. Some people use the shopping cart as an easy "save for later" place to park potential purchases that they're not yet committed to buying, while others do the digital equivalent of leaving the cereal box at the register. As the company selling said product or service, how do you get past these hurdles?

The same way B2B tech vendors do.

In a grocery store, you surely have used the free trial/ account option before. Except instead of a login and password, you simply say yes when the employee at the little kiosk asks if you'd like to try a free sample. On Amazon, you can watch a demo video of someone using or explaining the product or read through the reviews.

Why not upload a customer testimonial video for each

item you sell, then let the system automatically send that in an email? That would be far more engaging than the generic yet nagging reminder "You Have Items in Your Cart." That's like sending a customer who hasn't gotten back to you an email that says, "You Didn't Buy from Us."

Don't nag. Give them a compelling reason to return.

Selling to One → Selling to Few

A major development that typically occurs at this stage is your buyer bringing in the rest of the buying team. That "team" might consist of the buyer's significant other, as with the example from chapter two where the buyer wanted a new red sports car, then watched that dream go down the drain after a cold dose of reality from the frugal spouse. That team might simply be the buyer's boss, and the admin wants the owner to okay their choice of caterer for the end-of-year party. The team could be the buyer's employees, as in the case of bringing in a potential new hire to meet the team and then get the team's impression about whether to move forward with the hire. The team could be the executive committee, as with the golf course managers (before SynaTek found a way to take them out of the equation). The team could simply be the buyer's friend to whom they turn for advice: "I'm thinking about buying this. What do you think?" Whatever the case, you need to have tools and tactics ready to influence those individuals' respective cyclones, too.

That's right. Everything you just did to get to the mindset of evaluation with this one buyer? You need to do that for everyone else on their team. Everybody needs to be on board. Otherwise, your primary contact stays stuck in that cyclone, as the golf course superintendents did.

If you just broke into a panic at the thought of having to move along four or five people in their own cyclones just to get the sale closed for one person, congratulations! You are starting to understand the sheer massiveness of how complex sales and marketing is today. This is one of the primary reasons that research shows some fifty percent of sales reps never hit their sales goals. They're not bad salespeople; it's just that their companies use the old tools and work out of the old playbook.

You do have an advantage, since by the time you reach this cyclone you have an inside ally, but it's only an advantage if you're truly the remarkable choice. Your buyer may have been told to "get three quotes," but if they fall in love with your business, then they're going to push for you as their preferred provider. If, however, you're simply one of three good choices, then they won't be nearly as passionate about advocating on your behalf. You see, if they go off and come back with three more or less good choices, maybe they feel they've done their job and checked that box. But make no mistake about it: even if they've invited you to meet the rest of the buying team, until you are *the* choice in their mind, they aren't in the Rationalization cyclone. As long as you're one of few, they're still in the Evaluation cyclone, regardless of how many of their team you talk to. But the minute they take the next step and begin to back you over the other two choices, while technically there may be three providers, in their mind, there's really only one. When they do choose you, the choice becomes *personal to them.*

In that moment, they've created an attachment. You're the horse they're backing and they want to see you win. The more emotionally attached to you they are, the farther out on a limb they'll go to see you chosen. It becomes a matter of personal and professional pride at that point. In fact, hearkening back to the CEB-Google survey of three thousand B2B buyers we referenced in chapter two,

> The study shows that B2B purchases entail personal risk, not just corporate. Buyers fear losing time and effort if a purchase decision goes wrong, losing credibility if they make a recommendation for an unsuccessful purchase, and losing their job if they are responsible for a failure.[30]

If you win, the buyer looks like a genius who picked the winning lottery numbers; if you lose, they might face reprimand or even severer repercussions. The more they back you, the more they stand to lose.

Don't let 'em down.

---

30 Mindi Chahal, "B2B Branding: Where Is the Love?" Marketing Week, April 2, 2014, https://www.marketingweek.com/2014/04/02/b2b-branding-where-is-the-love.

Addressing the Rest of Your Buyers' Pain (or Pains)

Let's say your company designs, manufactures, and installs solar power systems for large industrial facilities. Your target buyer is the on-site engineer. Through your brilliant marketing strategy, the engineer loves you and is a vocal proponent of installing your system in their plant. "Great! If you'll just sign here . . ."

If only it were that easy.

The engineer has to get buy-in from the facilities manager, the operations manager, and the CFO and then get the final sign-off by the CEO. Any one of these people can veto the whole idea. They all have different—and for some things, conflicting—views, perspectives, responsibilities, personalities, beliefs, genetics, and more. Additionally, none of them care about how much the engineer wants the solar panels. Among them, the engineer is the metaphorical lowest man on the totem pole.

First, you don't want to leave this uphill battle to the engineer.

Second, your goal here isn't to wrangle a meeting with each of them so you can sell them on the idea of installing solar panels. You want to find their pain and calm their fears. You need to step into their shoes: what issue of theirs could your solar panels solve or could you mitigate?

The facilities manager doesn't care about solar panels one way or another. They just don't want installation to take forever or mess anything up in the process. You solve their objection by showing them your company's reverse timeline process: they pick a completion date and then you work backward to establish milestones. All of that goes into your software that automatically tracks work progress and updates the facilities manager via email. They're delighted.

One down.

On the other end, the operations manager is extremely concerned about the power system. They worry the panels won't provide enough power for an entire industrial site. You sit with them to go over energy usage for the last twelve months to identify peak demand, and then tell them that their system will be designed for 125 percent of that, "just to be sure."

Two down.

The CFO wants to cut down on utility costs and ensure that the system provides actual ROI. How fortunate that you just so happen to have actual usage reports with you showing before-and-after graphs of energy costs of other customers! What's more, you show them how you track each customer's usage monthly and send it to them in a convenient Excel spreadsheet that they can easily drop into their own financial reports.

Three down.

By now, you have serious momentum. If the plant engineer, facilities manager, operations manager, and CFO have all agreed to the idea, the CEO probably won't stand in the way; their endorsement is probably a formality. If you were just focused on the sale, you could get their nodding approval and go. But because you're smarter than that, you seize the opportunity to create an ally in the CEO. You discover that they like the idea of having a solar-powered facility because it demonstrates the company's green commitment.

Yes, you say, that's a motivating factor for many of your customers. That's why you create an environmental impact report for every project, designed to be distributed throughout the company and the community; you prepare a press release for local newspapers and industry publications, and after project completion, you create a professional video they can share on their website and social media that focuses on the specific green benefits they've provided the community by switching to solar power—would they like to watch the video from another customer's project? It's only three minutes long.

Would they!

THUNDERBOLT IT

After seeing some success, Julie emailed Sam a status update.

His quick reply:

Congratulations! You've begun getting your prospects into the Rationalization stage. This is where the sales process kicks in. Prospects have chosen you, and they're ready to talk about working together—including the relevant details of what that working relationship might look like. But this is also where a lot of companies make big mistakes. Remember, people make purchasing decisions emotionally and then rationalize those decisions. So, you'll hear them say things like "You got a verbal" or "We want to go with you; we just have to do our due diligence." These people have emotionally connected with your team and want to hire you—but they still need to justify it.

Chat soon!
—Sam

Elsewhere in the office, Bonnie and Jonathan were discussing their next moves. They knew their job at this stage was to help prospects get comfortable with all the contract terms, cover the details, and provide support for their decision. They looked at the current sales process and started to add in a few more features to help prospects continue to feel safe during Rationalization—and to encourage them to move toward signing.

They put each step of the sales process on a flow chart and added key pieces of content or touches with the sales team. In one of these touches, during Rationalization, they used to simply send over their ten-page proposal as soon as the prospect asked for it. This almost always triggered a review and at least two weeks of back and forth.

Bonnie suggested looking at the proposal and making sure it was simple and direct—and all about the potential client. They also wanted to add a video call to review the proposal with the prospect, instead of just dumping it on their desk. Then Jonathan scheduled time with each of his team members to ensure they understood the stages and were committed to following the overall sales process, including this change to the end of the buyer journey.

Amber Lee also worked with Bonnie and Jonathan to create email templates for each touchpoint in the sales process. Not only did this save the salespeople time, it also kept the Thunderbolt IT story consistent, no matter who was telling it. The templates were also designed to allow the salespeople to do some light personalization, to avoid coming off as cold or automated to their prospects.

Bonnie went a step further by creating and designing an advocacy program, giving Thunderbolt a formal way to activate happy clients and solicit their endorsements. These clients agreed not only to serve as references but also to send templated emails to prospects, suggesting that working with Thunderbolt would be a very smart move. Bonnie even gamified their participation by allowing them to earn points for every email, reference, review, case study, or video they helped with. The points were good for small prizes like Amazon gift cards or Thunderbolt swag—or discounts on services, if that better suited them. It was fun and functional, a win-win for everyone.

The next time Thunderbolt had a prospect in the Rationalization stage, the sales team requested help from the advocacy group. A Thunderbolt client sent this email to the prospect: "Don't even think about it. Hire the guys at Thunderbolt IT—they're the best!"

After so much positive feedback on the sales videos, Bonnie had the great idea to create a reference reel from these advocates' interviews. She thought this would limit the number of references advocates had to provide manually and shorten the sales cycle, as the salespeople could send the reference reel link *before* prospects asked for references. After implementing this plan, they found that, while it didn't get rid of reference requests completely, it did knock them down by fifty percent.

For the CFOs, Bonnie created an ROI model: a spreadsheet prospects could use to calculate the return of an investment with Thunderbolt IT. Julie created a video describing Thunderbolt's implementation process and how it helped ensure and optimize ROI. It was the perfect combination of tools and content.

After reviewing the effectiveness of their new sales tactics on what Bonnie had uncovered as a secret shopper, they all agreed that Thunderbolt IT now had the best sales experience among all their competitors.

But they also recognized that confidence doesn't make money; that only closed deals pay the bills. They knew there was data they could gain access to that would help them understand exactly (and in real time) how these improvements were working.

To validate that all their efforts were paying off, Bonnie and Jonathan began tracking the Rationalization data in a custom dashboard. They had set up similar dashboards for all the stages in their new Cyclonic Buyer Journey.

The data included some of the following numbers:

- Average days from verbal agreement to signed contract

- Percentage of deals requesting references
- Number of proposals submitted
- Average time viewing proposals
- Average number of people viewing proposals

They were excited as they watched those metrics begin to move in the right direction.

9

ON MY WAY TO PAY: THE CYCLONE OF DECISION-MAKING

There is never a good sale for Neiman-Marcus
unless it's a good buy for the customer.

—STANLEY MARCUS, *MINDING THE STORE*

A friend of ours got serious about her personal finances and decided to cut up all her credit cards, paying for everything in cash or with her debit card. While such financial discipline is commendable, it comes with its challenges. The first time Michelle traveled for business, she discovered this the hard way.

As she always did on such trips, after landing she took the airport shuttle to the car rental center. She discovered that the rental center was undergoing a major remodel, so the multiple rental offices had been moved to mobile trailers scattered on properties surrounding the rather large airport.

No big deal, Michelle thought. *I'll just use the same rental agency I always do and wait for their shuttle.*

She rode the minibus to the poorly lit lot, waited in line forever while the customers ahead of her ranted and raved about the exorbitant cost of neglecting to refuel their rental before returning it, and finally got her turn. She knew exactly what kind of car she wanted, knew precisely when she would return it, and knew she wanted full coverage insurance as she always did.

Everything was routine . . . until she handed the agent her card.

"Ma'am, is this a debit card?"

"Yes, it is."

"Ma'am, are you familiar with our debit card policy?"

"Ummm, no?"

"Okay, our policy is that we need your return flight information and two forms of ID, and we'll need to place a hold on your card for the entire amount of the rental, plus an additional $500 that will be refunded to you upon return."

"What!? That's ridiculous!"

"I'm sorry, ma'am, but that is our policy for debit cards. Would you like to continue with your rental?"

She was fuming. She stepped out of line, whipped out her phone, and looked up the debit card policies of two other major rental agencies. They were just as stringent. It was late, she was tired, she couldn't walk to any other sites, it would be another half hour before the shuttle looped around again, and she needed to be well rested for her business meeting the following day. She was stuck. She got back in line, waited again, then bitterly handed the same agent her card.

Upon returning home, Michelle furiously dug into the debit policies of every single national agency and found one who didn't have a draconian attitude: Alamo. On her next business trip, she tried them and had such a wonderful experience that she decided then and there that she would never use another agency. And for nearly a decade, she hasn't.

The one time an airport didn't have an Alamo desk, she used Uber!

Losing the Buyer in the Last Mile

It doesn't matter that the agencies' debit card policies made sense from a business perspective. After a string of debit card–related frauds and losses, companies began to enact harsh policies to protect themselves from further loss and to discourage customers from using debit cards altogether. That's a perfectly rational response to a major problem.

But that's operating from the seller's perspective.

From Michelle's vantage point, she had an awful experience that soured her on not only that agency but all other agencies. It didn't matter that she should have planned better and investigated their debit card policies beforehand. It didn't matter that she was the architect of her own mess. Like virtually every human being in the world, she blamed the company.

In the parlance of her cyclonic journey, because Michelle saw the agencies as commodities, she simply used the one she was most familiar with. She skipped the Education, Consideration, Evaluation, and Rationalization cyclones completely and went straight to the Decision-making cyclone based solely on convenience and familiarity.

If she'd still used credit cards, she would have handed the agent her plastic, signed the papers, picked up the keys, and forgotten about the whole thing as she had so many other unremarkable rental experiences over the course of her career. But the events that ensued after handing them a debit card shot her back to the Consideration cyclone *despite the fact that she completed her purchase.*

Ever wondered how many of your wins are actually losses?

How many customers have handed you their money while silently swearing to never use you again? That happens more frequently than you probably imagine. You've done it yourself at plenty of restaurants. Restaurateurs spend God knows how much money on advertising when their real problem isn't getting people in the door but getting them to come in again.

But have you ever stopped to question how many customers you've lost not because of bad service or a faulty product but because of your buyer's purchasing process? Michelle was fine with everything until she went to pay. Inside the transaction, everything went sideways.

The Way You Pay

Traditional retailers have long known the importance of the checkout or point-of-purchase experience. Offering other products at the cash register not only increases revenue; having magazines and novelty items also distracts the shopper from how long it's taking Grandma at the counter to dig through her coin purse to count out exact change.

Today, most big box retailers give their customers the choice between self-checkout and regular checkout. Some people love self-checkouts, especially when they're buying a personal item that they'd be embarrassed for a cashier to pick up and scan. For them, self-serve kiosks offer a degree of anonymity. Other people hate dealing with the frustration of "Please place item in bagging area . . . unexpected item in bagging area."

As we write this, Amazon's experiment with a cashierless store looks like a success so far. At Amazon Go, shoppers pick up whatever they like and walk right out the front doors. As they exit, Amazon Go charges the card they have on file and emails a confirmation. They have brilliantly eliminated the point of purchase altogether. There is no "friction" at checkout because it doesn't exist.

While Amazon Go may be at the forefront in the United States, China's BingoBox has more than three hundred cashierless stores in thirty cities throughout the Asian nation, with no plans to stop expansion.

Even though these companies make the news with their no-checkout experiment, for a few years now Walmart has quietly rolled out the same concept in many of its stores. With a Walmart app, shoppers can use their phone to scan their items, pay while standing in the middle of the aisle, and then walk out. In the same store, while Grandma stands in the checkout line, her son may be at the self-checkout as her granddaughter pays via mobile.

Speaking of online checkout, do you remember when virtually every e-commerce site waited until you got ready to check out, then made you set up a whole account with them to proceed? You had to provide your email (if not a phone number and mailing address) and create a password according to whatever security rules they had ("Must contain one uppercase and one lowercase alphanumeric sequence of no less than five characters and no more than sixteen, and must contain at least one of the following symbols . . ."). Then you had to wait for an email, click on the confirmation link, and then go back to login. All of these steps to buy a pair of socks. eBay, Apple, and other giant retailers finally figured out that they were losing millions in potential revenue because people didn't want to be bothered with the hassle. Apple updated its checkout screen to offer two options: one for returning customers and another for guests. For many shoppers, and especially first-timers, this gives them exactly the checkout experience they want. For returning customers, Amazon pioneered the one-click option. Like Amazon's physical counterpart, it completely eliminates the whole Decision-making cyclone (unless their card is declined; then it spins up their buying cyclone quite a bit).

Similarly, most hotels have also removed the Decision-making cyclone. Time was, you had to pay at the front desk before you checked out. Today, they swipe your card upon check-in and slip your bill under the door the morning you plan to leave. Business travelers everywhere rejoiced. They no longer had to budget extra time to wait in line behind some irate guest at the desk arguing about an extra bag of peanuts charged to their room.

Carside/curbside service has revolutionized the casual dining segment and delivered some brisk growth for brick-and-mortars. Jaron Waldman, former head of Apple's Geo division and now cofounder of Curbside, says that restaurants report between a forty-five percent and seventy-five percent increase in sales when they use curbside pickup in conjunction with a mobile app.[31]

31 Peggy Carouthers, "Why Curbside Pickup Is the New Drive Thru," QSR, November 16, 2017, https://www.qsrmagazine.com /content/why-curbside-pickup-new-drive-thru.

Imagine a fifty percent sales boost just from a new way to pay!

Purchase Should Be an Experience, Not a Transaction

Purchasing is not about your buyer finalizing their decision.

They have already made the decision. They've picked out their product or service. They know what they want; they just need to pay. But what will their payment experience look like? For Michelle, it felt like hell. For the vast majority of our purchases, it's an unremarkable event, nothing wonderful or awful. Just a plain vanilla, here's-my-money-here's-your-order transaction.

That's the word you need to key in on: transaction. You don't want your buyer's act of purchasing to be a transaction. You want it to be a remarkable experience, something worth remembering and retelling.

Like CD Baby.

Depending on your age, you might even remember CDs, but there was a time when if you wanted to share a large digital file (well, "large" for back then), you had to burn the data onto a CD and then physically mail it. Yes, even to the two of us now, it seems antiquated. If you're a millennial, it sounds like the Stone Age.

CD Baby's checkout experience was so remarkable that it still delights us to this day. When you bought music from their online store, here's the confirmation email you got:

Your CD has been gently taken from our CD Baby shelves with sterilized contamination-free gloves and placed onto a satin pillow. A team of 50 employees inspected your CD and polished it to make sure it was in the best possible condition before mailing. Our world-renowned packing specialist lit a local artisan candle and a hush fell over the crowd as he put your CD into the finest gold-lined box that money can buy. We all had a wonderful celebration afterwards and the whole party marched down the street to the post office where the entire town of Portland waved "Bon Voyage!" to your package, on its way to you, in our private CD Baby jet on this day.

We hope you had a wonderful time shopping at CD Baby. In commemoration, we have placed your picture on our wall as "Customer of the Year." We're all exhausted but can't wait for you to come back to CDBABY.COM!!

Thank you, thank you, thank you!

Sigh. . .

We miss you already. We'll be right here at store .cdbaby.com patiently awaiting your return.

All your friends at CD Baby

This jovial tone may not be appropriate if you run a funeral parlor and crematory, but focusing on the tone misses the bigger picture. CD Baby's checkout experience was such a delight that we're still talking and writing about it nearly *a decade later.*

Skipping the checkout line may be a novel experience now, but that won't last. Just like having the Internet on your phone used to elicit daily conversation, today, we take it for granted. In fact, someone who doesn't use a smartphone might be a topic of conversation. While tech or a gimmick might be a short-term answer to creating a remarkable experience during the sale, CD Baby's approach creates something so genuine and memorable that we still refer to it years later.

Offline, most retail checkout lines are boring and nondescript—plenty of junk with big profit margins to keep you occupied and hopefully earn more revenue. French cosmetics retailer Sephora, however, adds a little pizzazz. When the store isn't busy, you can walk right up to the centrally located checkout counter. When a queue begins to form, a twisting checkout line conveniently begins (or ends, depending on how you look at it) about four feet from the counter, much like an airport ticket line. But Sephora's queue is different from a ticketing line as well as other retailers' checkout lines. Instead of simply trying to stuff as much merchandise onto the shelves that form the queue, Sephora artfully designs theirs.

As an acquaintance of ours describes it,

> It's like a little maze organized into sections. The first category might be skincare, then eye care, and

then you make a turn and see lip stuff, then around another corner is the perfume. Each time you move ahead, there's a different section of things you're looking at. And everything is sample sized at $2 or maybe $3—definitely everything's less than $10, so it's really tempting. The shelves are shorter than at like a Walmart or somewhere else, so you don't feel squeezed in. The shelves are white and clean, everything's organized and pretty. You don't mind standing in line because it feels like you're still shopping and looking at stuff.

Then when you get to the front of the line, you don't have to wait long because they always have plenty of people. When the next checkout lady is open, they call you up and then ask if you have a Sephora card. I love going on my birthday because they give me a free gift! They always put your stuff in a pretty bag and say something nice. It's just a really nice experience.

When was the last time you heard someone refer to a checkout queue as "really tempting"? When was the last time you didn't "mind standing in line"? Sephora is surely making money on the cosmetics lining their maze, but they've found a way to have the best of both worlds. Their customer enjoys it, and some even look forward to the mystery of what's around the next turn.

When "Checkout" Takes Weeks (or Even Years)

The examples on the previous pages spoke to consumers' experiences.

What about longer B2B transactions?

In *Fire Your Sales Team Today*, we wrote about how our company screwed up a potential client's "checkout" experience. We had been approached by a business owner in the process of buying another company. He planned to merge the two and wanted a completely new identity that infused the best of both. Our business development guy (this was before we transformed those positions into "sales guides," one of the main points of that book) did a wonderful job of walking him through the different steps of our sales process (this was before we created cyclonic marketing, the whole point of this book).

In going through the final paperwork, our guy realized the client hadn't registered the domain for his new company name. Worried the straightforward domain name might already be taken, he jumped on GoDaddy and found to his relief that it was still available. As anyone well knows, registering a domain is relatively cheap and simple. That is, if someone else doesn't buy it first. If they do, then you have to buy it directly from the current owner, often a protracted process. To date, the most expensive domain award goes to "cars.com" for $872 million.[32] (That's not a

---

32   Joe Styler, "The Top 20 Most Expensive Domain Names," GoDaddy, July 24, 2017, https://www.godaddy.com/garage/the-top-20-most-expensive-domain-names/.

typo.) For years, "economist.com" didn't take you to the British magazine but a homemade page devoted to Alan Greenspan. If you wanted the website for the storied publication founded in 1843 and owned in part by the fabled Rothschild family, you had to put "the" in front of the address. Imagine how many readers throughout the Commonwealth expected to see the magazine's iconic red logo and were surprised to see a picture of the U.S. Chairman of the Federal Reserve instead.

Knowing stories like these, our team member quickly scooped up the web address for a three-year period. Excited to have scored this coup on behalf of the client, he emailed the CEO immediately: "I registered your domain name. I'll drop you an invoice to be reimbursed for the $45."

The CEO blew up—and so did our new deal.

You can appreciate the prospect's perspective. An agency with whom he hadn't even finalized an agreement was already buying things and then charging him without asking first. If we acted like this before he became our client, he might have reasoned, how much more aggressive and assuming would we be afterward?

Had we known about our employee's well-meaning but misguided intentions before he bought the domain, we would have asked the prospect first. Had we known about his purchase before he emailed the prospect, we might have told him to wait until the paperwork was signed and we were officially hired to act on the company's behalf—an "easier to get forgiveness" type of situation. Or we might have told him to gift the domain to the owner like this:

> In reviewing all the details of our agreement, I saw that your company's domain name was sitting out there in the open for anybody to claim. We rushed to buy it to make sure nobody else got it first. As a token of our goodwill, we'd like to give it to you at absolutely no charge in advance of finalizing our agreement; the three-year registration was only $45—an absolute steal.
>
> A "happy birthday to your new company," you might say!
>
> How would you like us to transfer the registration to you? If you have a GoDaddy account number already, it's very easy. If you use another service, no problem! I can coordinate with our in-house interactive manager to find the easiest way to get it into your hands.
>
> The important thing is that the perfect website address for your new company is now secure. One less thing to worry about!

Just framing it differently might have resulted in delighting the prospect instead of destroying the project. Forty-five dollars was peanuts against the revenue of the proposal, not to mention the potential revenue over the lifespan of our relationship.

After this event, you can be certain that we implemented the advice we're giving you now. In the last mile, you cannot rest on your laurels, secure in having won the sale. If anything, you have to be even more diligent. The closer a buyer gets to signing on the dotted line, the more they worry about whether it's the right decision. Every interaction gets microanalyzed. Any lingering fears are amplified. In the same survey we referenced for the data on B2B buyer's remorse, the author wrote, "Buyers are never 100% sure they are purchasing the right product. Regardless of their confident demeanor, on the inside they are experiencing fear, uncertainty, and doubt."[33]

In response, you need to microanalyze your processes around purchasing. Set boundaries and policies, especially for any prospect-facing interactions, for every team, from revenue generation to customer service.

Carrying a B2B Sale over the Last Mile

In the words of a late-night infomercial: "But wait, there's more!"

To complicate the purchasing situation further, you have to be sensitive to everyone composing "the buyer." In the previous chapter's solar panel example regarding the Evaluation cyclone, we spoke about what it looks like to influence the rest of the buyer team. After becoming the

---

33   Katie Bullard, "What Do B2B Buyers Want?" DiscoverOrg, https://discoverorg.com/blog/what-b2b-buyers-want/.

site engineer's one choice, you needed to then influence the CEO, CFO, operations manager, and facilities manager. If we continued with that example, we would need to talk about running the gauntlet with the "other rest" of the buyer team: the details people. Legal. Procurement. Accounting. An oversight committee. All those wonderful deal killers who make the best-laid plans of mice and men go awry.

As the hypothetical sales guide, you offered to go with the site engineer to each person's office. This not only saved the engineer having to persuade the higher-ups on his own but also let you quickly provide the information needed to address their pain.

You want to do the same thing in the Decision-making cyclone. The buyer team has made the decision to purchase; the details team just needs to vet the proposal for any potential issues. Here again, you want to be the one walking the contract through all the necessary departments. You don't want to leave it up to the engineer (or whoever your primary contact is) to provide the information they need. You don't want to leave the agreement to the mercy of the organization's internal bureaucracy. At every moment, you want to know exactly where it is, specifically who's reviewing it, and precisely what they're thinking.

Just like in the Evaluation cyclone, you want to be prepared for their objections, red flags, questions, and concerns. You want a library of options or demonstrable evidence ready to use that addresses their fears. If legal raises an issue, provide the number of a current client's attorney who had a similar question. You'll have that at the ready because you already talked to the other lawyer beforehand and got permission to use them as a reference. If procurement has a question, send them a case study outlining how another customer dealt with that very situation. If operations seems hesitant, send them the link to an interview you recorded with a technician from another customer's company. Then go one step further. What if the proposal needs to be reviewed by teams in multiple countries? For a relatively insignificant amount, you can have documents, case studies, video subtitles, and other materials translated into their native languages for their convenience.

Work hard to make their jobs easy.

THUNDERBOLT IT

"Julie, have you thought lately about how far you've come since our first coffee?" Sam asked.

"Often! Bonnie and Jonathan have become my dynamic duo. They're unstoppable!"

"That's how it should be in every company. Sales and marketing shouldn't be at odds with each other; rather, they should work together to create a seamless experience for the customer. I'm so glad you have that at Thunderbolt," he said.

"Me too," she noted. "Now we need to focus on getting people from Rationalization to—what? What do you call the next stage of the cyclone?"

Sam said, "It's called the Decision-making stage. It's what you've been working toward—when you get the signed paperwork, and the new customer becomes official. This is the toughest, yet most rewarding, stage: getting to yes. You simply close the deal and bring on the new client.

If the prospect's journey was designed and executed correctly, this stage should be where the results of all of your efforts manifest themselves."

"That echoes what Jonathan said the other day. He's a big believer that agreements and proposals are just confirmations of a deal already struck. He says that if his team has done their job, signing is simply a formality."

The mentor nodded. "I agree, but as Liam Neeson said in *The A-Team*, 'Overkill is underrated.' You still want to create a great experience for prospects in this cyclone, too."

Julie returned to the office. She, Bonnie, and Jonathan put their heads together.

Bonnie spoke up: "As the outsider, maybe this is a dumb question, but why are our contracts so dense? I've read through them, and I'd rather have another root canal. Do they have to be written so . . . I don't know—legal and technical?"

Julie frowned. "You know, Bonnie, I had an attorney draw up our agreement, and we've used him to add things here and there, but . . . you're right. If you're about to sign for a $400,000 contract, it doesn't make the prospect feel very safe to have pages and pages of legalese. I'll take on the task of working with our lawyer to simplify it."

Alone in her office again, Julie thought back to Sam's question about how far her team had come. She was more than encouraged about their progress—she was ecstatic. The synergy between sales and marketing; Amber Lee's enthusiasm; the sale team's buy-in; the new processes; the real-time data and dashboards; the videos, the email templates, and all the new, creative touchpoints . . . it was wonderful.

For the first time in years, she actually began looking forward to reviewing sales numbers.

10

THAT NEW CAR SMELL: THE CYCLONE OF DELIVERY (NEW BUYER)

*We are not in the coffee business serving people,
but in the people business serving coffee.*

—HOWARD SCHULTZ, FORMER CEO OF STARBUCKS

You need to wow your buyer the first time they buy.

If their experience with your service or project is anything less, it might be even harder to make another sale, much less to upsell or cross-sell. If they have an experience that meets only the bare minimum of their expectations, you might have won their purchase, but you didn't win their heart and soul.

It's like virtually every movie theater—if you've been to one, you've been to them all. When you get ready to go to the movies, you choose according to what's closest to the restaurant. You don't have affinity or loyalty to one in particular. The extent of your preferences ends at staying away from the worst of them.

Then you have Alamo Drafthouse Cinema.

You know those passive-aggressive PSAs that play just before a movie starts, featuring some cutesy animated figure and a voiceover warning you that you'll be kicked out of the theater if you're disruptive? Wouldn't it be nice if the theater actually did? Short of someone getting in a drunken brawl, they never do. They let the offenders sit through the entire movie, talking on their phone or throwing popcorn at the people in the rows below.

Can you imagine one of those PSAs going viral? Alamo Drafthouse's PSA on YouTube currently has more than 4.7 million views—of a warning to not talk during a movie.[34] What's more, they didn't even create something original; they simply play a voice mail left by an irate moviegoer who'd been thrown out, ahem, "asked to leave" their movie house for using her cell phone.

No children under six. No unaccompanied minors. No latecomers. No cell phones. No talking. No refunds.

---

34 *Don't Talk: Georgie from IT,* performed by Jackson Robert Scott (2017; Alamo Drafthouse, 2017), YouTube, https://youtu.be/ATr6HomDNQc.

Those are the rules at Alamo Drafthouse Cinema. Follow them and enjoy; fail and face the consequences. They don't play around.

Now, if you go in expecting to act like you do at any other theater and you then get thrown out, you will have a bad experience, as did the person who left the voice mail. If you're like the rest of the civilized citizenry and treat a movie theater as you would live theater, then you will absolutely love it. If you didn't know about the rules before, your expectations of a normal movie-watching experience will be blown away. If you did know but suspected that Alamo Drafthouse simply paid lip service to the idea (just like every other movie theater), you will be pleasantly surprised to see that they are as serious as advertised. If you truly love cinema, you'll never go anywhere else.

A Remarkable Experience

Some travelers feel the same way about Southwest Airlines. Like a movie theater, one airline is just about as bad as another. United has had a run of awful public relations incidents over the past several years, including the viral hit "United Breaks Guitars" and the video of the Chinese-American doctor being hauled out of the plane with blood running down his face (which, by the way, happened because some United crew members needed to fly at the last minute; Southwest employees would never dream of kicking a passenger off the plane just so they could have a seat).[35] Despite these PR nightmares, over-all customer satisfaction surveys usually place United as average or in the third quartile: "They may not be great, but some are worse." Southwest, by contrast, has done an amazing job of consistently exceeding new customers' expectations and reaffirming others'. From funny seatbelt buckle raps to saving a service dog's life, the stories of amazing customer service don't stop.

One of our friends had a remarkable experience with PODS, the moving and storage company. She would have to wait about three months from the time she moved out of one house and into another, so she needed to store all of her worldly possessions somewhere in the meantime. PODS to the rescue.

The driver arrived in the scheduled time window and presented himself at the door. He wasn't what she expected. When you think about "moving guys," you think about hulking men sweating profusely in ripped T-shirts and jeans. The gentleman at her door was dressed in a buttoned-down shirt, khakis, and polished work boots. She shook his remarkably clean hand, chatted for a moment, and then confirmed where she wanted the remarkably clean and bright white container and in which direction she wanted it to face.

When he went back to his remarkably clean and

35   Ben Mutzabaugh, "United 'Clarifies' That Flight 3411 Was Not Oversold,"
      USA Today, April 11, 2017, https://www.usatoday.com/story/travel/flights
      /todayinthesky/2017/04/11/united-clarifies-flight-3411-not-oversold/100331782/.

well-maintained truck, he took out a pair of black leather gloves (no wonder his hands were so clean) and then began the unloading operation. She said it was like watching something out of a sci-fi movie as he used a controller to have a mechanized steel frame pick up the entire container, maneuver it over to exactly where she'd said, detach itself, and then load itself back onto the flatbed.

Capture that image in your mind: a suburban mom with a million things to pack standing in her doorway watching a storage container being unloaded just as she would if she were in a movie theater. You don't have to have Southwest-type customer service to deliver something remarkable.

You Only Get One Shot at a First Impression

We've separated the cyclone of Delivery into two distinct buyer experiences—their first (this chapter) and then subsequent (next chapter)—because it reflects the psychology of your buyer.

The first time they make a purchase from you, they may have high hopes that you'll deliver the upstream additive to their production facility precisely on time or that your gizmo will perform as advertised. If you're a temp agency, you always want to deliver good placements, but it's especially important with a new client's first temp. If the temp is a complete disaster, what are the odds the client will blame the temp instead of you?

Until they see the evidence for themselves, they will still have a degree of anxiety. In many cases, that anxiety increases because now that they've bought from you, they're locked in. They bet on you to win the race, but now you have to perform. That's why their first experience with your product or service is so critical to long-term revenue generation.

Exceeding expectations should be every company's goal, but far too often companies fail to meet even minimum expectations. Take the case of a friend of a friend who got a free car rental upgrade to a Jaguar (not Michelle, in case you're wondering). When one of her Facebook friends asked how she liked it, she wrote, "I am so *not* a car person—yet I was underwhelmed with the Jaguar. Not zippy, not luxurious, not memorable."

The agency had rented her one of Jaguar's newish "entry luxury" models aimed at helping the legendary carmaker break into the mass market. While such an affordable luxury strategy may give Jaguar a win in volume, it definitely didn't deliver the remarkable experience this executive expected. (In fact, in the same thread, another friend asked her if the car in the photo was a Kia. It's pretty bad when people can't tell the difference between a Jag and an economy car.)

Brian Fravel, the vice president of marketing at online B2B sales enablement company Veelo, shared a story of how failing to wow initial customers seriously hurt the company:

I was part of a team that made the mistake of pushing a product to market simply to hit an arbitrary launch date. . . . As we moved closer and closer to the launch date, it became obvious [we] wouldn't be ready in time . . . we started taking out features so we could hit the launch date. We thought we could get away with a "version 1" product that would be "ok" and then launch a "version 2" shortly thereafter. . . . **We launched "version 1" on time, without not only differentiated features, but barely even some baseline features. The product failed** in the market and the whole program was canceled. . . . Within 12 months, competitors came to market with products like the one we had defined originally, and they were very successful.[36]

While B2B buyers may be more forgiving in judging your marketing, they're far less apt to give you a second chance if you screw up the first time around. With every buyer, having something remarkable or, in the words of the disappointed Jag renter, "memorable" is critical. If you can't at least meet their minimum expectations, stay out of the game until you're ready to be a serious player.

---

36 Garin Hess, "5 B2B Sales & Marketing Leaders Share Their Epic Fail Stories in the Spirit of FAILFAST17," Consensus, May 18, 2017, https://www.goconsensus.com /blog/5-b2b-sales-marketing-leaders-share-their-epic-fail-stories-in-the-spirit-of -failfast17/; emphasis added.

Remarkable Packaging

Alamo Drafthouse, PODS, and Southwest sell services; how do you wow a first-time buyer if you sell consumer products? We don't mean while they're shopping—they could be in any cyclone, from Education to Decision-making—but once they've bought the item itself? The CD Baby confirmation email we showed earlier is a great example for both the Decision-making and the Delivery cyclones; in the moment following a purchase, the line between the two blurs.

Here's a clear-cut example: buying the new iWhatever. Apple has set the standard for product packaging. Whether you buy a new Mac or the latest iPhone, unboxing is an event all in itself. Where most manufacturers just use the most efficient means necessary (think bubble wrap and Styrofoam peanuts) and then throw the instruction manual wherever in the shipping box it lands, Apple specially designs each product's packaging to be as sleek, minimalistic, and beautiful as the tech itself.

Ad agency Cole & Weber used wood to create the packaging for a holiday wine. Literally. They took a thick piece of pine log, milled the inside to the exact dimensions of a bottle of wine plus a customized box of matches and a greeting note. As they explained, "Not only did we create a great shipping container for the wine, but that container was the backdrop for a great holiday experience that could last beyond its opening."[37]

---

37 Cole & Weber, "Holiday Log," Ads of the World, March 22, 2012, https://www.adsoftheworld.com/media/direct/cole_weber_holiday_log.

The Sephora customer's experience from before also touched on this idea: "They always put your stuff in a pretty bag." While perhaps not as remarkable as Apple's product packaging or as novel as a milled piece of fresh-cut pine, it's still quite a nice experience and, importantly, makes a lasting impression on a first-time shopper.

Dollar Shave Club takes a different tack. Not only are the blades and other products delivered in custom-designed boxes, the packaging itself reflects the company's voice and messaging, such as the quotes on the blade boxes: "Scratch off lottery tickets, not your face" and "'I like shaving with a dull razor.'—No one, ever."

When Remarkable Delivery Takes Time

What if you don't have something immediately for your buyer? What if it takes time to create and deliver your product or service? Take a luxury home builder we worked with (not Rittenhouse, FYI), for example. A common anxiety the home builder heard from its clients was "I just don't know what's going on!" Creating email sequences, scheduling progress/status calls, and other such touch-points didn't seem to help. Evenings and weekends would still find the homeowners-to-be schlepping up to the construction site, looking around disappointedly, and then calling the contractor again.

We said, "Why don't you just buy a $49 webcam and place it at the site?"

They loved it. Their clients loved it. Their clients emailed the login and password to everyone. All their friends and family loved it. Additionally, since we put the login on the builder's website home page, it drove an influx of people who got to see their loved one's home being built right before their eyes, increasing the site's web traffic, search engine optimization, and number of opt-ins. For $49, you can't beat that kind of investment.

Just a few years ago, BMW rolled out a program at its Spartanburg, North Carolina, plant that lets customers watch their special-order X3 being manufactured. How cool to see your own custom car coming together! Brackley Boats out of Ontario does something similar with custom boat building and restoration. At the end of each day, they take pictures of their work and email the images to the respective owners. Day by day, boaters get to see their little dream come (back) to life. The clients constantly forward the pictures to their friends and family. Even though the clients of Brackley and BMW aren't physically present, they are absolutely emotionally invested the whole time.

Our web design team delivers an immediate wow by quickly prototyping a placeholder website, in some cases within a matter of days like they did for the Teazzers website we referenced earlier. The quick turnaround is impressive (especially if you've been on the client side of a website project), but the wow factor really comes from the client having something to look at, point to, and think about how much more remarkable their 2.0 website will look. Our team has taken a lengthy deliverable and found a way to quickly delight our clients while working toward the bigger goal.

IT consulting firm Uptake Digital welcomes new business clients by sending the primary contact an iPad preloaded with Uptake's monitoring app and the client's account information. Everybody loves free gizmos, but this one is an ongoing reminder to the client of Uptake's love as they use Uptake's app to check on Uptake's work.

Speaking of status updates, while charity: water isn't a business, it offers an effective example of how to immediately deliver some wow to donors (read: buyers) after they fork over their money. A donation to charity: water triggers an email (one of a series) that lets the donor know the current status of their chosen project, such as getting permits for a water system or training the local community on its care. The email also provides background information and data on the local region, the people, and charity: water's on-the-ground partners who are or will be installing the water system. Upon project completion, the nonprofit sends an email to all of the project's donors replete with pictures and GPS coordinates of the site.

Remarkable delivery, even if it takes time to fully deliver.

Create a Remarkable Moment

With a physical item, it's relatively easy to create a remarkable delivery experience, but it's a bit more challenging to create that same level of wow when selling company health-care insurance policies or corporate auditing services.

Or business revenue generation.

Much of our work isn't sexy. We love telling the war stories of Rittenhouse and Drucker & Scaccetti, but a lot of what we do is . . . quite frankly, boring. Cleaning up databases. Working with CRMs. Optimizing conversion rates. Creating a content marketing strategy. While we can point to these things to demonstrate a deliverable, they're not tangible. Instead, one of the small ways we welcome a new client is by sending them a jar of Marshmallow Fluff with an attached note that reads, "This is the last fluff you'll ever get from us." Nine times out of ten, it elicits a joking response from our clients and, more importantly, creates an emotional connection with our agency.

Plenty of larger companies have box seats at a stadium or bring their clients to a big event. That's not really what we're talking about here. You want to create a remarkable moment ASAP, not according to the Philadelphia Eagles' season schedule. It needs to be more than just sending them a baseball cap with your logo or a pen with your name. It needs to *mean* something.

Buy them a subscription to an industry journal or magazine—one that's relevant but not so prevalent that they already have a subscription of their own. If you really want to wow a new client, send them a copy of a relevant book that you personally recommend with a note why you think it will help them. Better yet, follow our example and write your own—or three!

Here's a thought: why not create a custom item to create a remarkable moment? Instead of the same boring hat with your logo, why not a hat with the client's name juxtaposed with your logo and the date to commemorate an event? There are probably twenty promotional product vendors within a mile of your office and dozens online, such as Vistaprint, who can put that image on literally thousands of individual items.

Or you could go online and create your own custom M&M'S package. You can choose up to three colors out of twenty-one, add your own image or pick from a gazillion clipart images, and then add your own text. Why not buy customized M&M'S printed with the names of the people on your buyer's team and then match their company colors?

Creating something remarkable doesn't necessarily need to be tangible. A consultant we know sells strictly online training products. But when a new client purchases an online course, the consultant's personal assistant instantly reaches out to them to schedule an unexpected fifteen-minute phone call between the consultant and the new customer. This delights the customer, of course, because they had no idea that they were going to get a one-on-one call with the consultant. Unsurprisingly, this consultant has one of the lowest cancellation rates among his industry peers. It also gives him the advantage of continually checking in with new subscribers to make sure his messaging stays on track and gives him insights into how his customer demographic may be changing.

A little bit of wow doesn't have to be ringside seats at Madison Square Garden. Like our Marshmallow Fluff or a fifteen-minute phone call, creating a remarkable moment just needs to show your buyer that they are important enough for you to go the extra mile as soon as they click "buy" or sign on the dotted line.

Table Stakes for Delivery

Most of our content in this chapter revolves around the overall customer experience. We made a conscious choice not to focus on examples about delivering amazing products or services.

We shouldn't have to. Designing your store, delivering incredible business strategy insights, configuring your e-commerce navigation, creating a high-quality widget, or cutting the perfect steak—whatever it takes to deliver a remarkable product or service to your buyer, you do it. Those are the table stakes in today's world, where the buyer holds the power and has dozens or thousands of other competitors to choose from.

In *Awesomely Simple*, author John Spence wrote, "If what you sell is not worth buying, no amount of good ideas, cool strategies, or slick marketing will help you."

Truer words were never spoken.

THUNDERBOLT IT

For the first time since they started meeting, Sam was late.

He apologized as he sat down in the booth across from her.

"I'm sorry I'm late, Julie. I was reading through everything you sent over this morning and got so engrossed, I lost track of time!"

Julie smiled. "It's not often you hear someone describe sales material as engrossing!"

"True! But it is. Your 'dynamic duo' have really created something amazing. I haven't missed an episode of *Thunderbolt IT TV* since you started. It feels like your company is really gaining some traction."

He dropped his voice. "But, Julie . . . you've completely overlooked a crucial aspect of your growth strategy."

The CEO felt the panic start to rise.

"Don't worry, though. Once you've successfully converted a prospect into a client, it's far, far easier to upsell and cross-sell. That's what your revenue plan is missing: more sales to existing customers."

She sat back in the booth. "You scared me, Sam. I thought we had really missed something."

"Oh, but you have, Julie. Think about all the time and effort you've put into chasing leads, people who don't know you. Now, think about your current clients, people who already know you and like you. If you reached out to the CIOs of the companies you're currently serving, would they take your call?"

"Of course they would. We're their IT partner."

"Have all of them bought all of the products and services that Thunderbolt IT provides?" he asked.

"No," Julie admitted.

"And yet, there are competitors of yours trying to get a meeting with them to sell them those products and services. They *wish* they had the access you do. Why not leverage your position as a trusted partner to market and sell like you do to prospects?"

By this time, Bonnie and Jonathan were used to Julie calling them into the conference room immediately after her return from the Bean Café. That day was no different.

Bonnie had a blank look. "Of course, this makes a ton of sense. We've been so focused on net new, we didn't really pay much attention to the current customers and the revenue opportunities there." She turned to Jonathan, VP of sales.

Jonathan shrugged. "We've never really thought about

selling to current clients. I don't even know if we have incentives in place for cross-selling."

Julie went to the whiteboard and uncapped a marker. "Well, then, let's figure out how to market and sell to people who already buy from us."

At the end of a two-hour session, they had a list of ideas.

First, they would start sending a monthly educational email to their existing client list, sharing new ideas in the industry and featuring a customer project success story. This would encourage other customers to engage with Thunderbolt on similar projects and allow Thunderbolt to have an ongoing conversation about new services with every client, every month.

Next, they wanted to get better feedback from customers on how they were doing. Instead of waiting for issues to arise, they thought about taking the proactive approach of issuing periodic customer satisfaction surveys. These surveys would not only alert them to potential trouble but also provide insights into how their clients used their products and services.

As far as customer support went, it was easy to see that clients were calling in regularly with the same set of questions. To make that experience better, they created a knowledge base and put it on their website; customer service reps could now direct callers to the appropriate knowledge base article. In no time, the number of calls dropped and customer satisfaction increased. As new questions were identified, new content for the knowledge base was created, and it grew into an online resource that was highly accessed and highly ranked on Google. This, in turn, drove new leads for Thunderbolt IT and made it easier for current customers to find answers to their questions.

Just like the sales team, the customer service team spent a lot of time sending emails to customers. Bonnie and Amber Lee worked to understand what those emails were for and created a set of email templates that made it easier for customer service to respond—also ensuring that the Thunderbolt IT story, tone, and service experience was consistent. These templates included suggestions, recommendations, and reminders around all the services Thunderbolt IT provided, which made Jonathan and the sales team very happy.

The following Thursday, Julie sat down across from Sam in their usual booth. After going over all those ideas, he looked up with a smile.

"Julie, congratulations! In just under a year, you've created a framework for helping your buyer through each of the eight stages in the Cyclonic Buyer Journey. All you need to do now is continue to review, analyze, and optimize what you've started. Now, there's only one step left."

She looked puzzled. "You know, you're as bad as a kid at bedtime: 'Just one more thing!'"

He laughed. "Yes, I am as bad as a child in many regards, but in this, you need the patience of an adult. Do you remember my third condition?"

"No, but hang on," she said, as she flipped through her notebook. "Okay, here it is: 'Don't change our priorities away from this stuff until we're hitting sales goals for four quarters in a row.'"

"Close. I said, 'Don't even *think* about changing priorities until you've hit your sales goals for four quarters in a row.'"

"Okay, you got me. The thought of pivoting or introducing something else may have crossed my mind once or twice."

"I'm sure it has. But don't seriously consider changing direction until you hit that milestone."

Julie said, "You don't have to worry, Sam. With the new growth engine we have inside our company, I'm actually excited about the future. I'm ready to start seeing the results of our marketing, sales, and customer service efforts."

He said, "Julie, I promise you'll be there before you know it. In the meantime, just focus on your eight stages, the eight individual cyclones and the big Cyclonic Buyer Journey, and on helping your buyers navigate their individual buyer journeys."

. . .

It took a little over two years of hard work, and more than one setback, but Julie discovered the truth behind Sam's third condition. Creating a revenue generation machine that included marketing, sales, and customer service was a long-term project and required a long-term investment. It was a marathon, not a sprint. While Thunderbolt IT had, at the beginning, experienced some benefits from engaging in this new approach to revenue growth, that was nothing compared to their revenue a year later—which, in turn, was eclipsed by their revenue the year after that.

Eventually, because Bonnie and Jonathan had incredible teams, Julie was able to step out of sales and marketing to focus on company strategy. Acquisitions, new technology, and reseller programs helped fuel even more growth.

The next morning, a package arrived, and when Julie opened it up, she found a bag of Bean Café dark roast (her favorite), a small bag of biscotti, and a mug with the words "Even the Longest Journey Starts with a Single Step." Inside the box, she found a note that simply read, "What's next? Warmly, Sam!"

Perhaps now it's time for my next chapter, Julie thought and then dialed Sam's number.

11

"ARE YOU A REWARDS MEMBER?": THE CYCLONE OF DELIVERY (ONGOING)

In marketing I've seen only one strategy that can't miss—
and that is to market to your best customers first,
your best prospects second, and the rest of the world last.

—JOHN ROMERO

Keith, a serial entrepreneur, wanted to buy a piece of urban real estate. Since the downstairs of the property he wanted was already leased to a small pizzeria, he thought about buying the pizzeria's lease or even buying the business outright.

While doing his due diligence on the shop, he asked the owner how they kept track of sales, inventory, financials, and so on. The old man reached under the pizza counter and pulled out a beat-up metal lockbox: "At the end of the day, I put the money from the cash register in here. On Mondays, I take it to the bank."

Classic minimalist.

Wanting to bring the pizzeria into at least the twentieth century, Keith began looking at restaurant point-of-sale systems. He then found Lavu, a vendor who offered such systems for specialized restaurants, including pizzerias. After doing a little self-educating, he decided it was exactly what he wanted.

To his gratification, it was as advertised: easy and convenient. He had everything loaded up and the workers trained in a couple of days. Right off the bat, it helped him make an important business decision. The original owner didn't have the pizzeria closing until 3:00 a.m. From the beginning, Keith had intended to eventually set a much earlier closing time—until he reviewed sales. Not only did they have business during those wee hours, but on weekends, sales from midnight to three accounted for more than half of daily revenue. His Lavu system paid for itself in that moment.

Lavu had a solid content marketing strategy and constantly sent out information on how to increase sales, use new features, and get more out of your current system. One day, Keith received an email from them about a flat-screen, wall-mounted menu that would integrate with his system. He immediately recognized that it would solve an ongoing annoyance that both his staff and his patrons had. The daily specials were written on a chalkboard that faced the counter. When customers got up to the counter, their back was naturally to the chalkboard—and naturally they always asked about the specials. Lavu's wall-screen menu would address a number of issues by—

- Doing a better job of drawing the customer's eye, thereby better promoting daily specials

- Helping more customers figure out their order before getting to the counter, saving time

- Keeping the line moving faster, especially for the lunch crowd, who were more likely to order the special

- Automating the task, allowing Keith or the manager to schedule the daily specials in batches ahead of time to be automatically posted, instead of having to remember to change them by hand every morning

- Eliminating the annoying need to buy chalk at random times throughout the year

- Enhancing the pizzeria's feel and helping Keith in his vision to transform it from a stodgy neighborhood establishment to a hip place for today's urban dweller

Of course he bought it.

Acquisition vs. Retention: Pointing Out the Obvious yet Absent

It's easier to keep a customer than to land a new one.

Everyone knows that. It's common sense. But Frederick Reichheld at consultancy Bain & Company (and author of the best seller *Loyalty Rules!*) did a little research to discover just how profitable customer retention is. In financial services, he found that a five percent increase in customer retention equated to a twenty-five percent increase in profit;[38] in other industries, it's been shown to equate to as much as a ninety-five percent increase.[39] Staggering.

In a Bain report, Reichheld wrote, "Chick-fil-A has so effectively mastered the economics of loyalty, it can afford to pay store operators double or triple its industry's average compensation and still give 10% of profits to charity."[40]

Keep that concept in mind while we pose the following question: what is B2B marketers' number one priority? Content marketing effectiveness. And what is the number one goal for B2B content marketing? Brand awareness.[41]

38   Frederick Reichheld, "Prescription for Cutting Costs," Bain & Company, October 25, 2001, http://www.bain.com/publications/articles/prescription-for-cutting-costs-bain-brief.aspx.

39   Amy Gallo, "The Value of Keeping the Right Customers," *Harvard Business Review,* October 29, 2014, https://hbr.org/2014/10/the-value-of-keeping-the-right-customers.

40   Frederick Reichheld, "Prescription for Cutting Costs," Bain & Company, October 25, 2001, http://www.bain.com/publications/articles/prescription-for-cutting-costs-bain-brief.aspx.

41   Content Marketing Institute and MarketingProfs, "2015 B2B Content Marketing: 2016 Benchmarks, Budgets, and Trends—North America," Content Marketing Institute and MarketingProfs, 2016, https://contentmarketinginstitute.com/wp-content/uploads/2015/09/2016_B2B_Report_Final.pdf

In fact, take a look at how B2B marketers ranked their priorities, from greatest to least:

1. Brand awareness

2. Lead generation

3. Engagement

4. Sales

5. Lead nurturing

6. Customer retention/loyalty

7. Customer evangelism

8. Upsell/cross-sell

Let's recap. Everyone agrees that customer retention (i.e., getting people who have already bought from you to buy from you again) is easier than customer acquisition (i.e., getting people who have not bought from you to buy from you for the first time). Everyone agrees that it's cheaper to land sales from past and current customers than to get a first-time sale.

Forgive us for belaboring the point, but just so we're crystal clear:

- Current customers = cheaper and easier
- New customers = harder and more expensive

But . . .

- Top three priorities = branding, leads, and engagement—a.k.a. selling to new customers
- Bottom three priorities = retention, evangelism, and upsells/cross-sells—a.k.a. selling to current customers

Does not compute.

That's because most companies still operate on the sales funnel model. Marketing gets as many people into the top of the funnel as possible, then gets as many of them to the bottom of the funnel as possible, then serves them up to the sales team. From that angle, yes, marketing to get as many new customers as possible makes sense. Handling existing clients is sales' job.

The salespeople, however, are almost always measured by how many new deals they close. Few companies have decent incentives for selling to existing customers. Anyone can do that, right? But wrestling a reluctant client into a years-long contract—*that's* worth paying for. And it's easier to let marketing communicate with past clients anyway.

Round and round the merry-go-round it goes.

This is why it's so important to merge sales and marketing. Siloed, they focus on their respective functional skills. Unified, they focus on what should be their real goals in the first place: revenue generation. From that perspective, focusing your time and budget on new customers instead of current ones doesn't make sense. You're spending more dollars to chase harder sales.

Buyers already in the cyclone of Delivery are easiest

to influence because they've already bought from you. You're a known commodity. If you didn't mess up their journey (as the rental car company did with Michelle), they already know, like, and trust you, as Keith did with Lavu. When Lavu sent an email featuring its wall-screen menu, he was already in the Awareness cyclone on his chalkboard problem: an issue, but one so minor it didn't warrant his attention. Upon receiving the email, though, Keith skipped the cyclones of Education, Consideration, Evaluation, and Rationalization in a matter of seconds to go straight to Decision-making.

With enterprise organizations or even government agencies and contracts, it's logistically easier to upsell and cross-sell because you're already a qualified or even pre-ferred vendor. The online freemium model (e.g., LinkedIn and Dropbox) exists because it's an easy way to get users to buy what those tech companies really sell: premium paid accounts.

If an upsell or cross-sell is easier than an initial sale, why don't more companies—especially established com-panies with a solid customer base—devote more of their attention and budget on this kind of marketing?

Don't make their mistake. Focus more on buyers already engaged.

Creating Community and Customer Loyalty

A few years ago a friend recommended me to be a member of the Tennessee Squire Association; it's kind of a Jack Daniel's fan club. A few weeks later I received in the mail an impressive certificate plus an actual deed to part of the Jack Daniel Distillery in Lynchburg, Tennessee . . . and dismissed it as a very clever marketing ploy. That is, until I received a K-1 to attach to my income tax return indicating I had a loss of 29 cents due to flood damage on my "property" in Lynchburg.

Then, I began getting letters from folks who lived in Lynchburg, like I was a real neighbor. There was one from a fellow who ran the local hardware store wanting to take horseweed worms from my property to use as fish bait. . . . My favorite came from a guy trying to raise a herd of Black Angus cows. He kept getting calves with white faces; he claimed he spotted a white-faced bull on my property and wrote me for ideas on how to correct the situation.[42]

As proud squires ourselves, we can attest that such letters from our Lynchburg "neighbors" are sometimes the highlight of our day. We still chuckle about the time we got a photograph of two guys holding up a dead raccoon,

---

42   Chip Bell, "You Don't Know Jack . . . or Do You?" LinkedIn, September 6, 2016, https://www.linkedin.com/pulse/you-dont-know-jackor-do-chip-bell.

accompanied by a letter that read, "Sorry! We accidentally stepped on your property while coon huntin'—but look at this beaut!" Jack Daniel's has created a whole world of make-believe that keeps us intrigued. We look forward to receiving this cleverly disguised advertising ploy. Ask yourself: when was the last time one of your buyers *enjoyed* hearing from you?

We wouldn't be surprised to hear that Jack Daniel's found inspiration in the J. Peterman Company of Seinfeld fame. It comes as a surprise to many that a real-world John Peterman exists who does indeed travel the world finding rare and unique items to sell through a mail-order catalog. Each "Owner's Manual" features an eclectic mix of items, from its iconic horseman's duster to Victorian nightgowns to British pub signs. In place of a professional photograph, each item is depicted as a watercolor. Instead of boring descriptions, the company (often John Peterman himself) writes a short story or anecdote around the item, such as this for a man's striped sweater:

Toulon, 1940.

Rows of 340-millimeter cannons sit unchallenged and idle in their defense of Côte d'Azur, awaiting enemies that refuse to arrive.

Brussels has fallen, Paris is in the crosshairs, and, here, it's pleasantly mild with a stiff breeze coming off the sea.

Since the big artillery aren't being fired, they need to be maintained—a greasy task indeed. So, the crew's attire begs the question . . .

Why such handsome sweaters?

In this, you're better suited to be strolling the promenade than cleaning those clunky ol' guns. The material breathes easy, like that air off the Med that keeps inviting a self-determined furlough.

The stripes make it easier to spot men overboard in the surf, but what about a well-disguised Matelot out on the town?

Dressed up with a jacket and nice trousers, it'll dodge the attention of any authorities looking to fish you out of the drink.

When night sets in, the sweater hugs tight against the chill—like the mademoiselle you could have on your arm during your walk on the Rade de Vignettes.

Striped Summer Sweater (No. 5654). Classic Marinière-patterned pullover. Moves nicely between Spring afternoons and Summer evenings. Pairs well with jeans, cleans up shorts and boat shoes. 100% cotton with soft woven pile, unlined. Imported.

Like the Tennessee Squire Association, J. Peterman weaves a captivating fiction. These stories create an emotional connection. It doesn't matter that we rationally know they aren't true. We feel something, just as we do with a story on a TV series or in a movie. We feel joy when the hero wins and sorrow when a beloved character dies. Jack Daniel's and J. Peterman don't create these worlds to drive more leads. They want to fascinate the people who already love them and strengthen their ties with those undying enthusiasts.

During the Delivery cyclone, you want your buyer to *feel* something.

Calling Disney World an amusement park is like calling the Ritz-Carlton a hotel: their competitors don't even play in the same league. Harley-Davidson recreated itself. It's no longer a motorcycle manufacturer; it's a lifestyle company. Like Harley-Davidson "H.O.G.s", there are people who get together on weekends because they share a love for another mode of transportation: the MINI Cooper. The car has grown into a symbol of a lifestyle of shared values. Jimmy Buffett has grown beyond music: "Parrotheads" identify with the laid-back beachcomber life his brand represents. These businesses do an amazing job of keeping their buyers engaged.

But you don't need a million-dollar company to create the same kind of ongoing experience. Gary Vaynerchuk turned his father's Shoppers Discount Liquors store into a multimillion-dollar company with a cultlike following via *Wine Library TV* on YouTube. Think of your local indie bookstore, a hipster coffee shop, the family-owned Italian restaurant around the corner, or the sellers at the weekend farmers' market. Precisely because of their size, these businesses create unique, inclusive experiences and even direct relationships with their customers. The Zingerman's restaurants and specialty food shops in Michigan provide a brilliant case study of how creating incredible experiences for their customers has led the group of businesses to become Ann Arbor institutions, resulting in eight-figure revenues. Zingerman's Community of Businesses was profiled in *Small Giants: Companies That Choose to Be Great Instead of Big*, a whole book dedicated to small businesses that have, among other things, deeply loyal customers.

It's easy to get people excited about motorcycles, margaritas, and Mediterranean olive oil. What do you do, though, when you have a business nobody wants to ever hear about, such as the impossible marketing challenge of owning a funeral home? How do you engage with former clients? It's not as if you can send them an email: "Happy one-year anniversary on your purchase! To thank you for your business, here's a 20% off coupon. Hope we see you again soon!"

Traditionally, these businesses have relied on word of mouth and (forgive us for saying it) repeat business. In tragic times, families instinctively turn to the one they know, like, and trust. If "Generic Family Name Funeral Home" took care of great-grandpa, then when great-grandma passes, you'll more likely than not go back. Funeral home "marketing" often stops at personalized pens and having their name in someone's obituary.

Why not record someone's memorial service, use a freelancer to create a beautiful tribute video, post it in an online album, then invite the family to share the social media link with others, especially those who weren't able to attend? Why not create a fund that benefits the loved one's favorite cause and invite everyone to make a donation? In the weeks leading up to the first year of the loved one's passing, why not reshare the album and video and encourage those who haven't yet given to do so? Then make the act of donation an event itself. Invite a representative of the cause or charity to attend a small ceremony at the funeral home with family and friends, and create a remarkable moment by giving them a check—then upload *that* video to be shared on everyone's social media. Keep it going by tracking how their donations are impacting others' lives. It becomes a living, continual memorial to their loved one, echoing charity: water's approach that we spoke of in the previous chapter. Funeral directors already know how to be sensitive, sympathetic, and comforting from years—often generations—of helping families through a loved one's passing. They just need to take that wealth of experience and continue comforting people in the months and years that follow.

Turning from a literally morbid topic, let's look at a dull business in the B2B space. Aside from transcribing tax law by hand, can you imagine anything more boring than finding defects in computer code? If you run a software testing company, how do you create a wonderful experience for your software developing clients? Sure, you can create great content about how to do a better job of finding bugs or how to prevent them, but that kind of thing is Marketing 101. Every company should be continually educating their customers. Here, we're aiming higher: how do you create a remarkable experience so they love you?

Global App Testing found a way.

Companies often host "hackathon" events for computer programmers where teams compete on a real-world business or tech challenge. Testers, on the other hand, have traditionally been the red-headed stepchild in software development. Nobody ever does anything to call attention to them, much less celebrate their contribution. To rectify this inequity, London-based crowdsourced testing company Global App Testing created the nonprofit Testathon, "a hackathon for testers," and facilitates three-day events around the world, from San Francisco to São Paulo to St. Petersburg, sponsored by such client-partners as Facebook, Spotify, and Dropbox.

How much do testers love it? In interviews after the Stockholm Testathon, attendees' responses included "I think it's great. It's shocking that it hasn't happened before!"; "You just basically spend all day playing; it's absolutely amazing"; and even "This is the best day of my life!" Global App Testing took something seen as boring and created a whole excited community that fosters relationships with testing professionals.

You see, it doesn't matter what industry you work in or what size your company is, because it's not about you anyway—it's about your relationship with your buyer and their relationship with you.

Find New Ways to Be Remarkable

A family-owned equipment rental company retained our agency to help find a way to grow its business. That in itself speaks volumes. Every company has to guard against entropy and continually question "the way it's always been done." Family companies are especially prone to this because changing anything can be construed as a personal judgment against the family members who originally built the business.

This company operated the same way as virtually every one of its area competitors. A customer would park in front of the office entrance, wait in line, inform the clerk what machine they wanted, wait until it was ready, get back in their truck, drive around to the loading dock, help load the equipment, sign the paperwork, get back in their truck, and finally leave. The whole process took about a half hour.

We did some digging into their data. As is the case in nearly every company, about eighty percent of their sales came from roughly twenty percent of their customers. Even with the rest, though, the vast majority were repeat customers. Like Amazon's one-click idea, we thought, *Why not cut out all the unnecessary repetition?* What if they created a "VIP customer list" that kept payment method and other information on file and listed authorized users.

These VIP customers could call ahead and say what they needed to pick up. The warehouse would have the equipment cleaned, oiled, and waiting at the loading dock. When the customer arrived, they would drive directly to the back, watch their rental be loaded into the back of their truck, and sign the papers that the dock worker handed to them through their truck window.

A process that formerly took thirty minutes now took three.

Time is money, especially for contractors. Not only did the rental company's existing clients love the new "flyby pickup" program, but they raved about it to all their contractor buddies. The next time those contractors were sitting in another equipment rental company's lobby, what do you think was going through their mind?

"You Want Fries with That?": The Cross-Sell

Keith's flat-screen menu purchase is a classic example of a cross-sell. Again, why companies don't pour their money and efforts into their own Keiths, we'll never understand.

E-commerce retailers have it easy on this front. If you view one product, the site automatically suggests complementary products—"Frequently bought together"—or competing products—"Customers also viewed these items." Cross-selling online is simply a matter of code.

What about offline retailers? We once heard a consultant in the consumer packaged goods industry talk about his pet peeve: grocery stores designed to shelve products solely by category. "If I'm buying spaghetti noodles, chances are I'm making spaghetti. If I'm buying cereal, I'm going to drink it with milk. If I'm buying birthday candles, I certainly need a birthday cake. So why do I have to walk all the way to the other side of the store to buy complementary items *they know I'm going to buy together!?*"

(Guy was passionate about his grocery stores.)

More and more retailers have begun pushing their frontline employees to cross-sell merchandise. Old Navy, for example, began a program to train sales associates to act more like high-end clothiers, helping shoppers piece together a whole ensemble instead of the traditional "Is there something I can help you with today?" approach.

These consumer examples come easily enough because they're so common. You know what's not common? A company salesperson picking up the phone to talk to an existing client. Even if they do, many such efforts are geared more toward retaining current clients rather than trying to identify other ways they could provide additional products or services.

How many times have your own customers bought from a competitor because they simply didn't know that you also offered x, y, and z? Here's a better question: if your company has multiple divisions, do they share their customer information with each other? If you work at midsize company, the answer is probably no; if an enterprise-size company, almost certainly no. In fact, often employees in one division don't even understand the additional services their employer offers in another.

Then there's the counterexample of Moyer Indoor |Outdoor, an outstanding case study of an entire business model built on cross-selling. This residential services provider offers HVAC, plumbing, pest control, security, pool care, lawn maintenance, and more. After you become a Moyer customer for one service, they begin introducing you to the family of other services. Instead of expanding geographically, they've found growth simply by offering their own customers more of what they already need.

"Would You Like to Upgrade Today?": The Upsell

To really understand the potential of upselling your buyers, you need to read *Priceless* by William Poundstone, a profoundly insightful academic book on consumers' perception of value. One of the big reveals is just how much the concept of numeric anchoring (some also call it the "contrast effect") plays into how we judge a literal or figurative price tag. Plenty of luxury stores carry an item with a breathtaking price—not because they really expect to sell it but to make everything else seem cheaper by comparison. Retailers have done this for years, of course. Plenty offer a good deal on something in their window front to entice shoppers to come in, then suggest an item that's "only a little more" but with a much fatter margin.

Airlines have taken this concept to the extreme. Major carriers continue to slash prices to win the ticket sale ("Look how much cheaper we can get it through this airline!"), then turn around and nickel-and-dime you to death. They've even started "upselling" the soft drinks and peanuts on some flights. This isn't upselling as much as it's hidden fees. Maybe they should just give the tickets away for free—everything else would certainly seem cheaper by comparison.

You don't want your buyer's journey riddled with unpleasant surprises and gotcha fees. As an aside, one of the main reasons for online shopping cart abandonment is the delivery fee, hidden until the last second. The designers' thinking behind this is that, like a real-world shopper, by the time the buyer gets to checkout, they're already committed and emotionally connected to the item, so they go ahead and eat whatever surprise costs pop up. This psychology doesn't work in digital retail because (a) it's missing the emotional connection that comes with handling a tangible item and (b) it's far easier for an anonymous shopper to simply leave a webpage than it is to walk away from a retail counter while the cashier and other shoppers watch you.

Upsells should be experienced as a convenient add-on or even an indulgent luxury. Take the example of the modular office provider North Forest. As part of its service agreement, company reps schedule a quarterly review with each lessee to reassess their space needs. If the lessee has grown and needs to lease additional office modules, the upsell is part of a natural conversation.

The online freemium model has become the classic upsell. Gmail, Dropbox, iCloud, YouTube, and thousands of mobile apps hook you with a great no-cost product, then offer the more robust premium options at increasingly higher prices. The same could be said for SaaS (software as a service) companies. When your buyer wants to add more users, extra licenses, or additional seats, they trigger the upsell naturally—no effort needed on your part. Upselling is built into these companies' DNA.

More and more businesses are trying to incorporate this easy upsell approach into their business model by offering subscription services and then offering upsell opportunities within that framework. Thirty years ago, no one would ever dream that one day millions of people would have a membership subscription for a car wash, car ownership, HVAC service, roofing service, razor blades, perfume, IT services, and even dog treats. Today, not only do these subscription services exist, but many offer multiple packages or levels of service. An introductory membership package offers the basics (i.e., a low-risk offer); when the buyer sees that the company meets (or, ideally, exceeds) their expectations, they often upgrade.

Jill Konrath, author of *Selling to Big Companies*, once wrote, "You need to think small, not big. Basically, your goal should be to get an initial project that gives you a chance to prove your value and establish a relationship with someone in the company."

That's all Enterprise Financial Consulting and Rittenhouse Builders did: they found a way to create something remarkable for their buyers at a small scale for a shot at the upsell. It's our own strategy with our enterprise clients like Staples and Fitbit, and one that virtually every company can copy.

Create something remarkable, then keep finding new ways to do it again.

12

"I DEMAND TO SPEAK WITH A MANAGER!": THE CYCLONE OF DELIVERY (TROUBLE)

The first step in business growth is to
keep the customers you've already got!

—ROY H. WILLIAMS

Do you remember when some grocery stores or even restaurants had a wall of shame? They would tape a picture of someone's bounced check behind the cash register with "Do NOT Take Checks From These People!!!" written in bold letters for the world to see.

UberConference did the digital equivalent to one of its customers.

Jung had used the web-based conferencing app for over a year prior to the date in question. One of UberConference's primary differentiators is not requiring a PIN. Just dial the number and you're immediately added to the conference. As a self-employed consultant, Jung loved it. Not only did it eliminate one of the hated elements of conferencing (the dreaded million-digit PIN), but the service also wasn't branded, unlike its main competitor: "This service provided by FreeConferenceCall.com!" He used it all the time, for calls with existing clients and sales prospects. While Jung was distracted by health problems, the credit card attached to his account expired. He saw the automatic emails, but putting in the numbers of a new card for an online app was at the bottom of his priorities.

Imagine his surprise when he dialed in to speak with a prospect to finish negotiating a $65,000 project and heard, "We're sorry. This account holder has been suspended due to nonpayment. Goodbye."

You could hear his heart hit the floor. He silently prayed that the message had only played because he called from his primary phone listed with the service. He ran into the other room and grabbed his wife's cell phone. Same message. He tried a landline also not tied to the service. Same message.

No, he didn't get to the executive in time to provide a different call-in number. Yes, the $65,000 prospect heard the message when she dialed in. No, she did not return his subsequent calls or his emails.

It was Jung's fault that he failed to update his card. His buyer was whirling around the Decision-making cyclone. As we said in chapter nine, buyers are especially fearful here, looking for any hint of trouble. He should have been more cognizant of that, just like our own agency's employee should been before buying and invoicing someone who wasn't even our client. Jung and our employee both screwed up and lost the sale.

Who did Jung blame? UberConference.

He railed that if UberConference had played a different message such as "We're sorry. The number you dialed is unavailable. If you feel you have reached this recording in error—" or something along those lines that the prospect would have assumed there was a technical problem and emailed him to ask for a different number. He would have wrapped up the project and landed a cool sixty-five Gs.

It doesn't matter that Jung was in the wrong; Uber-Conference's message severely diminished his loyalty. He continued to use them because he had the number incorporated into a number of his marketing assets, but he found himself back in the Evaluating cyclone, comparing the service to other providers, fully intending to switch.

This story has a happy ending. UberConference listened. They took his advice and changed their recording for suspended accounts to "I'm sorry you're having problems. Please check your conference information or try again later." Jung appreciated that they acknowledged their error. He even took some of the responsibility on himself for neglecting such an important detail.

UberConference held on to Jung, but just barely.

They could have avoided the issue altogether by simply walking through the buyer journey and asking, "Does our current policy for dealing with problem customers help win them or lose them?"

Obviously, their message for suspended accounts didn't instill a sense of loyalty. While nonpayment and past-due accounts are a continual thorn in the side of many businesses, your company needs an explicit policy and a detailed process for dealing with such situations. Have you seen the cost of new customer acquisition? It's cheaper to keep existing customers. Some portion of existing customers will have a problem. If you immediately throw them under the bus the moment they don't fit your ideal, you can't be surprised when your other customers question how much your company actually cares about its relationship with them.

Hear us when we say this: customer service should be folded into your marketing team (which, again, should be folded in with your sales team to create a revenue generation department). Not only can your buyer's experience with customer service make or break their loyalty, but it can make or break your chances with other buyers. Go Google "bad customer service" and you'll be reading and watching posts for days. Those are easy examples. We're not here to warn you about the dangers of such but to inspire you to find opportunities to experience the golden counterexample of awesome and revenue-driving buyer interactions.

Let's start with a legend.

Refunds and Returns

Has a change in your return policy ever made the news, much less received national coverage? That was the case when L.L.Bean changed its approach. Before, it would replace anything the customer wanted, no matter how long ago it had been purchased. Unfortunately, the years seemed to finally catch up, and the company ended its policy in 2018, citing customer abuse. Its new policy is still quite generous though: "If you are not 100% satisfied with one of our products, you may return it within one year of purchase for a refund." Plus, this policy applies only for items bought after February 9, 2018. If you bought a duffel bag on February 8, it's covered for life.

That's legendary.

Speaking of luggage, have you ever had an airline damage yours? Sure you have. Business travelers have come to expect it and simply budget for a new bag every year (or every quarter, if you're a real road warrior). Last chapter we talked about Southwest's amazing customer service; we get to point to them again here. A friend of ours had just bought a new duffel bag. On his very first flight using it, the baggage handlers (or somebody) partially ripped the handle. Normally, he would just chalk it up to the reality of air travel, but he was angry about it this time. He went to the Southwest agent, prepared for a fight. Instead, the agent asked if he would like to select a replacement.

Wait. What?

The agent took him to a room filled with brand-new luggage and asked him to select the one he felt matched his damaged luggage most closely. Still dubious, he pointed at a duffel bag on a nearby shelf. The agent took it down, opened it for his inspection, then asked him, "Would you like me to help you transfer your belongings, or would you prefer to do it yourself?" He walked out of the airport with a brand-new duffel bag and a newfound love for Southwest.

Plenty of companies want to provide great customer service—right up until their customer doesn't fit inside their neat little box of "How the Customer Is Supposed to Act." We remember when it took an act of Congress to get out of a cell phone contract. We've been on the receiving end of taking back some piece of merchandise and having to fill out a return form that asked for our life story as the customer service rep suspiciously eyed us from the other end of the counter. Don't even get us started on what it's like to ask an airline ticket agent for help; you might as well walk instead of fly.

On the flipside, plenty of shoppers go to Nordstrom

precisely because of its wonderful return policy. (Remember the story about Nordstrom allowing a customer to return car tires, despite the fact that Nordstrom doesn't even sell them?)[43] Taking this concept to the extreme, online retailer Zappos has created an entire business model on the strength of its return policy. Customers buy multiple pairs of shoes, fully intending on returning many of them or all if they don't like them. No problem. Zappos lets you go online, print out a prepaid shipping label, tape it to the box, and drop it in the mail. Done—no muss, no fuss.

Owning Up to Your Own Failures

In the chapter on the Rationalization mindset, we talked about addressing problems or things that your product couldn't do. Your buyer may have already thought about the issue, read about it from a user review, or heard about it from a colleague. Facing such concerns head-on gives you more credibility and makes you look like the hero.

When you mess up, fess up.

In a widely read post on Signal v. Noise, an industry blog by Basecamp, Ian Hall related how the previous night his Netflix stream had messed up. As the provider of

---

43   Paul Frichtl, "Yes, THAT Nordstrom Tire Story," Alaska Airlines, October 5, 2015, https://blog.alaskaair.com/alaska-airlines/people/nordstrom-tire-story/.

an online app himself, he knew that such encoding problems happen all the time. He didn't think about it again.

But the next morning he woke up to an email from Netflix apologizing for the trouble and giving him three percent off his monthly bill. He wrote, "Now while 3% of my bill isn't really going to add up, it makes me FEEL 100x better. And here I am gurgling over my feelings and the attention Netflix pays to their customers."

In the same vein, there's a great mini case study about how Kyle Racki, CEO of SaaS company Proposify, dealt with a Twitter-shaming user. The user had a legitimate issue: Proposify's code screwed up while the small business owner was putting together a proposal for his first international client. At 2:00 a.m. He was justifiably angry.

While we wouldn't suggest copying the CEO's reply Tweet—"Hi [user] sorry for the issues you're having. Do you want support to reach out to help or just looking to publicly shame us?"—he did write an excellent email, to which the problem customer responded with this:

> I sent off my frustration the only way I know will get a response, via social media. In truth, it's a dick move, to go public on a frustration. I should know better. . . .
>
> Yet you took the time to email me. Tell me some of my ideas were good. Admit that you're working on some issues, that Proposify is not perfect. You didn't make any excuses, not one. . . .

You have a promoter in me. The product will always get better but the service, that's embedded in the people that run the brand.

Honestly, thank you for such a kind response and sorry for being such an ass Kyle.[44]

Despite the CEO's testy tweet, he turned a problematic user into a self-proclaimed promoter who went back on Twitter to rave about Proposify's customer service.

When we call customer service problems "opportunities," it's not semantics. It's make-or-break time. If you respond well to issues and especially legitimate complaints about product or service failures, you earn those glowing reviews (that have now made their way into a business book). If you fail, you can't be surprised when you get blasted on social media and user forums, forfeiting the opportunity to ever work with anyone who sees the post.

---

44   Emphasis added.

13

READING THE TEA LEAVES: A VISION OF THE FUTURE

Plans do not predict the future.

—MICHAEL GERBER

Even though we published *Fire Your Sales Team Today* in 2012, an excerpt from the preface still holds a relevant story and, truthfully, the origins of why we kept expanding our business offerings and for what eventually became our understanding of cyclonic marketing:

This book had its beginning after one fateful client meeting on a snowy day in the winter of 2007. The owner of a $10 million manufacturing firm had called us into his office to review the performance of his marketing program.

When we heard he wanted to "fire us," we were perplexed.

"Fire us?" we asked the entrepreneur. "The new marketing program we created for your business has improved the number of qualified leads from thirty a month to well over one hundred per month—why would you want to fire us?"

He responded very simply: "Revenue has not increased at all."

We asked, "Since leads are not an issue anymore, perhaps instead of firing us, you should allow us to spend some time helping you uncover why your sales team isn't converting those leads into revenue, and then help them fix that problem?" . . .

Before long, it became clear that the sales team was the main issue. This company employed eight salespeople who were responsible for bringing in new clients and handling orders from current clients. Of the eight, six never made their monthly quotas and the top salesperson was always the business owner. There was no sales process in place, so despite tripling the number of opportunities, the sales team could not keep up with the lead flow and, frankly, felt overwhelmed with the dramatic increase in work.

Over the next 120 days, we embarked on a mission to understand all aspects of the team's sales challenges.

What we learned was that sales and marketing, traditionally separated in business management, are no longer two different functions within a company. This is primarily because both of these critical processes center on the prospect. To serve the prospect effectively and convert that prospect into a customer, sales and marketing need to be a single, linear process that orchestrates a seamless series of communications directly to the prospect.

That was over a decade ago. We thought the collapse of the imaginary (or sometimes very literal) wall between sales and marketing would have been well underway by now. Unfortunately, this is still more novel than normal. In HubSpot's "2017 State of Inbound" report from surveying six thousand professional marketers, only forty-four percent say there's even a "general" alignment between the two departments.[45]

Wow.

On the other side of the spectrum, a number of more progressive companies now have standing service-level agreements between their sales and marketing teams, including twenty-two percent of those surveyed marketers. While each team may still sit in their own silos, they're at least committed to aligning their efforts.

---

45 HubSpot, "State of Inbound 2017," HubSpot, 2017, https://cdn2.hubspot
.net/hubfs/53/assets/soi/2017/global/State%20of%20Inbound%202017
.pdf?t=1529949369593&__hstc=20629287.c7d35e684e957dd90b062331c03
776a0.1464898340195.1529947084818.1529949375423.9&
__hssc=20629287.4.1529949375423&__hsfp=3622431204.

This, however, is just the beginning of what the future will look like.

Part of the McKinsey quote we presented in chapter two bears repeating:

> The research reinforced our belief in the importance not only of aligning all elements of marketing—strategy, spending, channel management, and message—with the journey that consumers undertake when they make purchasing decisions but also of integrating those elements across the organization.[46]

Customer service, operations, finance, IT—any touchpoint that any prospect, buyer, client, user, or anyone external to your organization experiences in any way whatsoever contributes to how people perceive you. How they perceive you directly impacts your top-line revenue.

Your buyer's journey is too important to leave to sales and marketing.

The Many Roles of the Chief Revenue Officer

The future of sales and marketing is a complete dissolution of both, with the responsibilities brought under the role of the chief revenue officer (CRO), as has already

---

46 David Court, Dave Elzinga, Susan Mulder, and Ole Jorgen Vetvik, "The Consumer Decision Journey," McKinsey & Company, June 2009, https://www.mckinsey.com/business-functions/marketing-and-sales /our-insights/the-consumer-decision-journey.

happened at the *Los Angeles Times*, Marketo, DocuSign, *Wired* magazine, Rackspace, and SolarCity (acquired by Tesla), among others.

The CRO is ultimately responsible for the company's revenue growth. They're not a glorified VP of marketing or of sales; they have a foot in both of those camps, as well as a finger in operations, IT, finance, and anything else that affects top-line revenue. Besides creating the systems and processes for generating revenue, they also work day in and day out to execute, optimize, integrate, and scale them across the entire company.

This role is both strategic and tactical. A CRO has to be great both in the boardroom and in the field. They talk to prospects, participate in the sales process, and see which pieces of the puzzle fit and how to make everything work like a well-oiled machine. Most importantly, they are the architect of the entire buyer journey, from Pre-awareness to Delivery. As such, an effective CRO is necessarily collaborative. They can't design, build, and optimize the revenue generation process across the whole length and breadth of the customer experience without working to cocreate the solutions with the finance, delivery, production, and executive teams.

Revenue is everyone's goal, but the CRO is the quarterback.

They have to gauge both subjective information—consumers' changing tastes and preferences—and the hard metrics that drive the business. They must be data driven to know which numbers matter and how to glean insights from them. At the same time, they need to know how to dig deeper into miscommunication between teams, customer service complaints, individual sales representatives' performances, product recalls, and negative online reviews (to name just a few of the issues on their plate) to understand a buyer's psychology driving their decisions.

If that weren't enough, a great CRO is also pragmatic. They understand how to balance the short term against the long term. They know how to embrace disruptive technology and how to use it as yet another tactic in influencing their buyer's cyclones. They have a good grasp of how to transition their company from old-school thinking into the new paradigm as they prepare for the long term, but not at a pace so quick as to seriously harm the company in the short term.

It's also been reported that some even walk on water.

The Rise of the CRO

The same year *Fire Your Sales Team Today* came out, *Forbes* published an article titled "The CEO's New Secret Weapon: The Chief Revenue Officer" written by Marketo's then CRO, Paul Albright. We imagine that, like us, Paul thought the market would force the shift to happen faster. At least it has some real momentum now.

But why? Why now? What's changed?

One of the main reasons is the complexity of the

tactics required to drive the buyer journey, remove buyers' frictions, and influence buyers through their cyclones. The tactics we list in the appendix include close to one hundred marketing, sales, and customer service actions. The metrics we list that every company needs to track include more than forty separate key performance indicators (KPIs). No mortal man or woman could possibly handle all of this on their own. Creating the necessary assets to execute those applications and collect the data behind those KPIs is daunting enough, not to mention that the daily, weekly, monthly, quarterly, and annual tracking of those KPIs is a full-time job in itself.

The data now available requires someone (or, depending on the size of your company, an entire team) to collect, track, benchmark, analyze, and report on the data, in addition to finding ways to improve the KPIs. The complexity of your buyer's journey coupled with the sheer volume of data you should be collecting is driving the growth of another professional role: revenue data analyst.

But what's fueling the future perhaps more than these other contributing factors are the toolsets now available. CRMs as well as sales force and marketing automation platforms have evolved in their ability to affect revenue. Full-scope customer engagement platforms including sales trends, marketing data, attribution models, customer usage behavior, issues, support, conversations, and churn data all provide new levels of analytics and insights that eliminate much of the guesswork in revenue generation, allowing it to become more measurable, objective, and data driven.

Rules, Regulations, and Ruin

Gary Vaynerchuk said, "Marketers ruin everything."

It's true.

Once upon a time, checking the mail was a pleasant experience. Today, people sort their mail over the garbage can. Anything that looks remotely salesy goes in, unopened. The stuff that looks somewhat legitimate gets opened—and then promptly round-filed too. Getting a phone call used to be a pleasant experience. Telemarketing ruined that to the point that governments in many countries passed laws with do-not-call lists.

"You've got mail!" used to feel like hitting the lottery. Now we have apps to filter the good from the bad (the digital equivalent of handing your mail to someone to stand over the trash can for you). Hearing a text notification used to mean something important was happening. Then marketers found us there, too. When was the last time you got excited about a text?

In December 2003, the United States passed the CAN-SPAM Act that, despite its name, was one of the very first (and still one of the very weakest) anti-spam laws. In June 2014, Canada turned on CASL, the Canadian anti-spam law. In May 2018, Europe turned on its far stricter version, the General Data Protection Regulation or GDPR. (You may recall getting one or two million emails regarding "Updates to Our Privacy Policy" around that time.)

Getting a direct message on LinkedIn was neat for a while, and then those lazy or desperate (funny how often those two go hand in hand) sales and marketing people got on there. Now, plenty of professionals don't even bother checking their LinkedIn inbox because it's just another repository for spam.

This doesn't even begin to cover consumer privacy laws and user data.

All of these regulations are going to eventually clear the middle field. Your marketing media will come down to two types: mass advertising like TV, radio, and billboards, or buyer-initiated connections, such as social media follows or requesting specific information.

The days of mass email blasts, mass LinkedIn messaging, and mass telemarketing will soon come to an end. The more technology enables communication, the more it also enables its own regulation. At some point in the future, the ability to even cold-call will be a thing of the past. (We know we'd certainly vote for it today.)

This means marketers, sales teams, and revenue generation specialists are going to have to work harder to create shorter, more direct connections between the people who want to buy and the people who can help them. Your content must be better so that prospects are willing to jump through as many opt-in hoops as the regulatory agencies require. Furthermore, revenue teams need to already have better policies on how to handle, store, access, and secure consumers' personal information.

The complexity is only going to get worse.

This doesn't make sales and marketing harder—it just makes *bad* sales and marketing harder. Smart sales and marketing professionals who genuinely want to help their clients, who respect their customers, who want a great experience for their users, and who are truly committed to doing something remarkable in the world . . .

We will not only survive but *thrive*.

TACTICS, ANALYTICS, AND TECHNOLOGY

Our prospects don't buy like they used to. That's why your marketing and sales tactics don't work like they used to. That's why the funnel doesn't represent the buyer journey like it used to. People don't simply find you, connect with you, and buy from you. Today, the buyer journey is chaotic, influenced by massive amounts of content, a steady flow of social posts, peers who have opinions . . . Your prospects are more confused than ever.

The prospect's Decision-making process takes longer, includes more people, and is much more complex than before. You might have experienced this in your own business. Longer sales cycles, lower close rates, deals lost at the last minute, prospects who ask more questions, and more uncertainty in the sales process are all clues that the world has changed.

The traditional sales funnel, which was created in the 1890s and has been in place since, is no longer representative of the buyer journey we described above. We're replacing it with the Cyclonic Buyer Journey™ model, which better illustrates the volatility, complexity, and uncertainty associated with the way people buy today.

We're also using this same model to bring clarity, strategy, and direction to marketing, sales, and customer service teams. By mapping marketing-, sales-, and service-related tactics, you'll know how and when to execute to better influence your prospects along each stage. By mapping data and dashboards to these new stages, you'll gain the insights you need to improve revenue generation. By mapping technology solutions to these new buyer journey stages, you'll automate and optimize Delivery—and overall company performance—more quickly, effectively, and economically. This is how companies will build revenue generation machines for their companies in 2019 and beyond.

A Tactics Map for the New Cyclonic Buyer Journey™

Here are the marketing and sales tactics you should consider if influencing your prospects at each stage is part of your go-to-market, revenue generation, or company growth strategies. Along the way, you might notice that tactics appear in multiple stages. There are certain tactics that are appropriate for prospects in a variety of stages. Lead nurturing, for example, is an effective tactic in almost every stage.

When tactics do appear in different stages, it might also mean they require deployment adjustments to ensure they are appropriately designed for the specific stage, persona, and company offering. Here are many of the commonly used tactics—but this is, in no way, a comprehensive list.

PRE-AWARENESS

- Account-based marketing (includes data clean and append, connect emails and engagement content, social and ongoing nurturing)
- Cold email marketing campaigns (purchased list or acquired list)
- Paid social media advertising
- Social media content creation and publication
- Banner advertising
- Retargeting banner ads
- Content syndication

- Affiliate marketing campaigns

- Influencer marketing

- Content publication on targeted sites/properties

- Events, tradeshows, and conferences—including speaking at these events, which can drive significant improvements in lead generation and position your company as a thought leader, as opposed to simply an exhibitor or attendee

- The traditional (but not generally recommended) print, mail, and cold-calling campaigns

- Graders and assessments to uncover issues the prospect doesn't know they have

AWARENESS

- Organic search engine optimization (SEO)

- Paid AdWords on search engines

- Website design

- Website pillar pages (for search)

- Conversion rate optimization (CRO)

- Visitor experience optimization on the website

- Content publication

- Social media marketing

- Content marketing—the production of disruptive, educational, and compelling content (persona-appropriate varieties and formats, with an emphasis on video, podcasts, and interactive content)

- Events, tradeshows, and conferences

- Blogging and guest blogging

- Email marketing

- Affiliate marketing

- Lead scoring

EDUCATION

- Content marketing (very heavy in this stage)
- Podcasting
- Video marketing
- Infographics
- Lead nurturing
- Email marketing
- Website design
- Website pillar pages (for Education)
- Chat for conversion
- Chat for intent
- Chat for Education and questions
- CRO
- Webinars
- Live educational events
  (company-specific, like INBOUND)
- Blogging and guest blogging
- Influencer marketing
- Advocacy (people telling other people)
- Lead scoring

CONSIDERATION

- Influencer marketing
- Blogging and guest blogging
- Video marketing—customer stories
- Paid social media advertising
- Content publication on social media
- Content syndication

- Content marketing (make or buy content, in-house or outsourced content)
- Case studies and success stories
- Advocacy (people telling other people)
- Lead scoring

EVALUATION *(Typically where marketing hands off to sales)*

- Website design
- Content marketing (Evaluation content, comparisons, proposal templates, questions to ask)
- Case studies and success stories
- Lead nurturing
- Email marketing
- Reviews
- Sales process design
- Content for the sales team
- Email templates for the sales team
- Sales training
- Sales coaching
- Lead scoring

RATIONALIZATION

- Sales process
- Sales email templates
- Advocacy
- References
- Reference reel (video)
- ROI models

- Delivery content

DECISION-MAKING

- Sales process
- Proposals
- Recommendation slide decks
- Contracts and agreements

ONGOING DELIVERY

- Advocacy and references
- Customer surveys
- Active referral program
- Knowledge base creation (for customer service)
- Upsell and cross-sell customer marketing programs
- Customer service communication (email templates)

A Dashboard Map for the New Cyclonic Buyer Journey™

Here are the marketing, sales, and customer service KPIs you should consider if measuring performance at each stage is part of your go-to-market, revenue generation, or company growth strategies. Each of these recommended data packages can be turned into a dashboard to provide easy monitoring daily, weekly, and monthly.

One important takeaway in this section is that tracking and measuring is just part of the puzzle. You should be planning on using data to gain insight that allows you to optimize high-performing tactics, test performance for challenging tactics, and shutter tactics that don't perform over time.

PRE-AWARENESS

- Total available market
- Total targeted accounts and total targeted individuals in those accounts
- Connect rate on targeted individuals
- Engagement rate on targeted individuals
- Conversion rate from engaged individuals to sales opportunities
- Click-through rates on emails sent
- Page visits from emails or social outreach
- Content downloads from emails or social shares; this usually equals the engagement rate above

- Answer rates to sales calls
- Call durations

AWARENESS

- Website visitors
- Site-wide conversion rate
- Net new contacts added to the database
- Social reach, followers, connections, and friends
- Conversion rate of visitors to sales opportunities
- Visitors from organic search
- SQLs from organic search

EDUCATION

- CTA button conversion rates (this month vs. last month)
- Landing page conversion rates (this month vs. last month)
- Blog subscribers (this month vs. last month)
- Webinar registrants (this month vs. last month)
- Webinar attendees (this month vs. last month)
- Conversion rate of registrants to attendees
  (this month vs. last month)
- Top five performing video assets
  (views, this month vs. last month)
- Video channel subscribers (this month vs. last month)
- Podcast subscribers (this month vs. last month)
- Podcast downloads (this month vs. last month)
- Top five performing CTAs/offers (clicks this month vs. last
  month AND leads generated this month vs. last month)
- SQLs from Education assets (this month vs. last month)

- Sales opportunities/leads from Education assets
  (this month vs. last month)
- New customers who viewed Education assets
  (this month vs. last month)

CONSIDERATION

- Percentage of highly qualified leads out of total leads,
  based on lead score
- Number of SQLs
- Conversion rate of marketing-qualified leads
  (MQLs) to SQLs
- General educational email click-through and email open rates
- Lead nurturing click-through and open rates, individual lead
  nurture emails, campaign nurture metrics and aggregated
  lead nurture metrics

EVALUATION *(Typically where marketing hands off to sales)*

- Conversion rate of SQLs to sales opportunities
- Open and click-through rates on sales sent emails
- Conversion rates on sales opportunities to
  proposals/agreements submitted
- Number of downloads of Evaluation content
  (this month vs. last month)
- Click-through rates on Evaluation CTA buttons
- Conversion rates on Evaluation landing pages
- Conversion rate of prospects from Evaluation
  to Rationalization stages

RATIONALIZATION

- Days from verbal to signed contract
- Percentage of submitted proposals that ask for references
- Conversion rate of prospects in Rationalization to final decision (yes or no)
- Proposal views, time viewing proposals, number of people viewing proposals

DECISION-MAKING

- Close rate on proposals/agreements submitted
- Average length of the sales cycle
- Average dollar value of new customers
- New revenue vs. new revenue goals

ONGOING DELIVERY

- Net promoter score
- Number of referenceable customers
- Percentage of customers who are advocates (write reviews)
- Percentage of customers who buy multiple product or service lines
- Renewal rate or churn rate
- Number of referral-based leads

A Technology Map for the New Cyclonic Buyer Journey™

With over seven thousand marketing and sales software applications out there, knowing which ones are right for you is crucial. These tools are an important ingredient for efficient execution of the tactics above and key to the installation of a repeatable, predictable, and scalable revenue-generation machine at your company.

One important takeaway in this section is that these tools alone will not solve your revenue challenges. In fact, these options should be the final step associated with building a revenue-generation machine. Software is only the answer after processes, systems, and methodologies have been implemented; then, the software can help automate and drive efficiencies.

PLATFORM/FOUNDATION TECH

TIER 1
Small business–level requirements

- HubSpot
- SharpSpring
- Infusionsoft
- Zoho

TIER 2
Midmarket and enterprise-level requirements

- HubSpot

- Marketo
- Pardot
- Eloqua
- Zendesk
- Salesforce.com
- Databox

PRE-AWARENESS

- ReachForce
- Demandbase
- Engagio
- Terminus
- EverString
- Outbrain

AWARENESS

- SEMrush
- Moz
- Unbounce
- BuzzSumo
- Bizible
- Full Circle Insights

EDUCATION

- Wistia
- Vidyard
- Drift
- Atomic Reach

- Powtoon
- Uberflip
- Ceros

CONSIDERATION

- Seventh Sense
- Conversica
- Drift
- Hushly
- Velocify
- Bizible
- Accent Technologies

EVALUATION *(Typically where marketing hands off to sales)*

- LinkedIn
- Journey Sales
- Drift
- SalesLoft
- Costello
- Yesware

RATIONALIZATION

- Excel
- Vidyard
- VisualizeROI
- SnapApp
- Showpad

DECISION-MAKING

- Proposify
- PandaDoc
- DocuSign

ONGOING DELIVERY

- Influitive
- Advocately
- SurveyMonkey

INDEX

E

eBay, 4, 174

e-books, 106, 140

e-commerce. *See* online retail

Economic Policy Institute, 73

economist.com (domain name), 181

educational content. *See* content

Education Cyclone

Buyer's intent in, 26t

for buying a car, 29, 31

content of education efforts, 100–102

dashboard for, 261–262

Enterprise Financial Consulting (EFC), 90–91, 92, 93–94

explained, 105–106

free webinars, 94–95, 96

helping buyer understand their pain/problem, 93

magazine ads, 91, 92

providing information on how to address buyer's pain, 100–101

reciprocity and genuine educational material in, 96–100

responsible departments in, 26t

Sarbanes-Oxley Act compliance and, 90–92

skipping the, 136

SynaTek (fertilizer for golf courses) and, 131–132

tactics, 257

technology tools, 265–266

true aim of education and, 92–93

video university, 106–108

EFC. *See* Enterprise Financial Consulting (EFC)

Eloqua, 265

email(s)

anti-spam laws, 250–251

automated nurture campaigns, in Awareness Cyclone, 85

to customer who has shamed you on social media, 240–241

educational, to current clients, 207

Thunderbolt IT's customer service, 208

email addresses

collected during Awareness Cyclone, 85

for references, 154

email marketing, 255, 256, 257, 258

email templates, 165, 208, 258, 259

emotions

appealing to, in Rationalization Cyclone, 147

buying behavior, 21–22

connection in Ongoing Delivery Cyclone, 220–221

emotive marketing messages, 21–22

Engagio, 265

Enron, 89, 90

Enterprise Financial Consulting (EFC), 90–91, 92, 93–96, 99, 134–135, 137, 231

Equifax, 54

equipment rental company, 225–226

Ernst & Young, 90, 91

Ersek, Barrett, 113–114, 115

Etsy, 4

Europe, anti-spam law in, 250–251

Evaluation Cyclone

being "remarkable," 132, 137, 141, 142

S

U

ABOUT THE AUTHORS

Eric Keiles and Mike Lieberman are lifelong marketing professionals and seasoned entrepreneurs. Friends since grade school, they decided to start a business together in 2003: Square 2 Marketing. Eric successfully ran a number of closely related marketing businesses, and Mike spent his career working for large corporates like D&B and Xerox. Because of their perspective, vision, and thought leadership around the massive changes affecting marketing sales and customer service, they saw the need for a change in traditional approaches years before it became an accepted fact. They captured their unique approach to marketing in their first book, *Reality Marketing Revolution* (2008), and then led the charge to align both sales and marketing into one single team in the widely acclaimed *Fire Your Sales Team Today* (2012).

As their vision broadened, so, too, did the services Square 2 provided. Today, they have clients all over the world and focus passionately on helping their clients with revenue generation, which includes strategy, tactics, metrics, and technology in marketing, sales, and customer service execution at their clients' businesses. Their clients span large companies like Staples and Fitbit to middle market companies with aggressive growth goals like Tru-Methods, Gliffy, Drucker & Scaccetti, and TierPoint.

Both Mike and Eric are regular speakers, thought leaders, and authors who are steadfast in sharing their approach with anyone who values building a scalable, repeatable, and predictable revenue generation machine for their company.

Made in the USA
Middletown, DE
21 September 2019